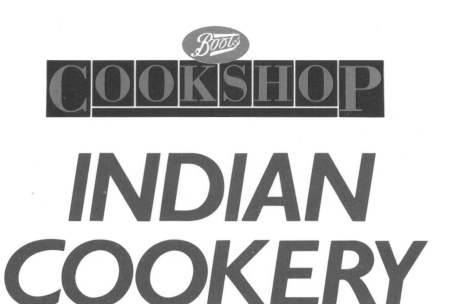

INDIAN COOKERY

COOKSHOP
INDIAN COOKERY

Khalid Aziz

Front cover photography by Dave Jordan
Inside photography: pages 16, 29, 33, 37, 41, 45, 47, 49,
53, 65, 67 and 69 by Dave Jordan; pages 11, 12, 21, 55, 56
and 59 by Bob Komar; pages 15, 19, 23, 24, 26, 30, 35,
39, 43, 52, 63, 71 and 73 by John Lee; pages 13, 16 and 75
by Mick Dean

Published 1986 on behalf of
The Boots Company Plc Nottingham England
by Hamlyn Publishing
Bridge House, London Road, Twickenham, Middlesex,
England

Text first published under the title
Step by Step Guide to Indian Cooking

ISBN 0 600 32613 6

Set in 10/11 Monophoto Gills Sans Light by
Servis Filmsetting Ltd, Manchester, England

Printed in Italy

Front cover photograph shows
Tandoori Chicken (page 22) and Palao rice (page 57)

Contents

Useful Facts & Figures

Notes on metrication

In this book quantities are given in metric and Imperial measures. Exact conversion from Imperial to metric measures does not usually give very convenient working quantities and so the metric measures have been rounded off into units of 25 grams. The table below shows the recommended equivalents.

Ounces	Approx g to nearest whole figure	Recommended conversion to nearest unit of 25
1	28	25
2	57	50
3	85	75
4	113	100
5	142	150
6	170	175
7	198	200
8	227	225
9	255	250
10	283	275
11	312	300
12	340	350
13	368	375
14	396	400
15	425	425
16 (1 lb)	454	450
17	482	475
18	510	500
19	539	550
20 (1¼ lb)	567	575

Note When converting quantities over 20 oz first add the appropriate figures in the centre column, then adjust to the nearest unit of 25. As a general guide, 1 kg (1000 g) equals 2.2 lb or about 2 lb 3 oz. This method of conversion gives good results in nearly all cases, although in certain pastry and cake recipes a more accurate conversion is necessary to produce a balanced recipe.

Liquid measures

Liquid measures The millilitre has been used in this book and the following table gives a few examples.

Imperial	Approx ml to nearest whole figure	Recommended ml
¼ pint	142	150 ml
½ pint	283	300 ml
¾ pint	425	450 ml
1 pint	567	600 ml
1½ pints	851	900 ml
1¾ pints	992	1000 ml (1 litre)

Spoon measures All spoon measures given in this book are level unless otherwise stated.

Can sizes At present, cans are marked with the exact (usually to the nearest whole number) metric equivalent of the Imperial weight of the contents, so we have followed this practice when giving can sizes.

Oven temperatures

The table below gives recommended equivalents.

	°C	°F	Gas
Very cool	110	225	¼
	120	250	½
Cool	140	275	1
	150	300	2
Moderate	160	325	3
	180	350	4
Moderately hot	190	375	5
	200	400	6
Hot	220	425	7
	230	450	8
Very hot	240	475	9

Note *When making any of the recipes in this book, only follow one set of measures as they are not interchangeable.*

Introduction

To anyone setting out for the first time to cook Indian food, there appears to be a myriad of regional variations with which one has to cope both in the type of dishes and the names of the ingredients used therein. Here you will find favourite recipes from all parts of India.

Making Yogurt

Yogurt is basically milk that has been turned sour by the action of various bacteria. In theory, as these bacteria multiply very quickly, it is only necessary to add a starter dose of the bacteria in the form of some already made bacteria from a shop yogurt and after a while you will have your own. In practice, as many of you who have tried will know, it is not quite as simple as that. This

Clockwise from top left: *fresh root ginger, garlic, mint sprig, curry leaves, fenugreek leaves and coriander leaves*

is because there exist in the air, and in the milk, several other kinds of bacteria, all of which are equally capable of multiplying. So the first step in making successful yogurt is to boil the milk, and leave it to boil for about three or four minutes. This kills off any bacteria that are liable to vie with the yogurt bacteria.

Thus we have prepared a breeding ground free of competitions for the yogurt bacteria. All living organisms have an optimum temperature at which they live best; yogurt bacteria are no exception to this rule and herein lies the secret of good yogurt-making. Once you have boiled the milk you must allow it to cool, and all you need to do is to add the starter dose of yogurt. But this is where most people make their mistake; if you add the yogurt when the milk is too hot you will find that after leaving the milk to stand for the requisite twelve hours you will have an excessive amount of watery whey and a lumpy, cheese-like substance at the bottom of the pot. This yogurt is not suitable for cooking or eating! The golden rule is: 'If in doubt, allow to cool'; it is far better to add the starter yogurt at a lower temperature than one too high. All you need to do then is to set the milk in a warm place in your kitchen where it is not likely to be disturbed for twelve hours. If you have never made yogurt before, I would advise you to start off with just a pint of milk although you will find that some of the recipes (especially those which are from the north of India) require greater quantities than this.

Cooking Utensils

Much has been made of the various cooking utensils which are used in the Indian cuisine but in fact you will find that the utensils are available in any western kitchen. For curries, all you need is a heavy iron pot and a wooden spoon with which to stir.

In some of the recipes I have mentioned the use of a liquidiser. Whilst this speeds matters greatly, it is by no means essential, and a little hard pounding with a pestle and mortar will achieve the same results, albeit less speedily.

In nearly every case where a specific Indian utensil is used I have found that there is a corresponding western one, and it is the latter which I have mentioned.

Cooking Rice

The cooking of rice seems to be another aspect of Indian cooking which Western housewives regard as a problem. One hears so many stories of how ordinary boiled rice has turned out as a jellied mass which takes hours to scrape off the saucepan that it is easy to believe that one has to be born within the shadow of the Taj-Mahal before one can produce perfect rice. Needless to say, this is not the case as long as a simple rule is observed, that is, always start with good quality rice. By good rice I mean the most expensive Basmati rice that you can buy – it is false economy to buy Patna rice unless you want to make rice pudding! When you have obtained the Basmati rice, all you have to do is to add the correct quantity (usually one cup of dry rice per person), to double the volume of boiling water and then boil until the rice has softened and there is no hard centre to each grain. Drain off the excess water and transfer the rice to a covered dish and put into a hot oven for 30 minutes. You will now have perfect snow white fluffy rice with every grain separate.

Spices

The appreciation of spices and their various combinations is an acquired art, and can only be achieved after many, many years of studied blending, cooking and tasting. However, it must be stressed from the very start that the word spicing does not apply solely to how hot the dish is but to its flavour, and as I have said before, it is the flavour that one should be aiming at when cooking an Indian dish. It would be helpful to go through some of the spices and to point out their various functions.

Coriander Seeds (*Dhania*) Coriander is used in three ways: either as the whole seeds; as powder; or as the leaves of the sprouted seed. The powder is more generally used both for flavouring curries and in the preparation of

Clockwise from top left: *dried limes, dried Indian apricots, tamarind (middle), black beans (whole and split), red lentils and brown lentils*

Clockwise from top left: *black peppercorns, cloves, saffron strands, sesame seeds, mustard seeds and white and black cumin seeds*

garam masala. The green leaves are used in the minced meat for koftas and kebabs or they can be used as a garnish.

Cumin Seeds (_Zeera_) Used whole in rice and bread. Ground seeds are used in curry dishes.

Chilli Powder (_Lal Mirch_) This is the dynamite that imparts the hotness to most Indian food. Use with care!

Tamarind (_Imli_) The pod of the tropical tamarind tree, used crushed to produce a bitter flavour in curries.

Fenugreek (_Methi_) Used with fish and some meat dishes, mainly to hide smells. Hence its use with seafood!

Turmeric (_Haldi_) This is the powdered root of a plant which grows in India. It is famous for its bright yellow colouring. When used in curries it colours the sauce a deep red.

Most of these spices and the various other ingredients both fresh and dried, are available at good supermarkets but any which you cannot obtain will probably be found in smaller Indian stores. A number of these stores found in larger cities operate mail order departments for those customers who live in the provinces.

Poppadums

Even the relative novice at Indian cuisine will know what poppadums are. Essentially the poppadum is a crisp form of bread made from chick-pea flour. I have not included a recipe for poppadums for although they seem a simple dish, they are incredibly difficult to make.

You will find that the poppadums you buy from the delicatessen are about four inches in diameter. After frying they should be double this in size. It is essential to keep the oil clean. The poppadums will be quite dusty and the dust will spoil the oil so before cooking, tap each raw poppadum to get rid of the dust. The temperature of the oil is critical. A piece of poppadum should sizzle immediately when dropped in if the oil is at the correct temperature. Use a large frying pan of medium depth and fill it with vegetable oil to just less than an inch below the brim. Heat gently and keep testing the temperature with pieces of poppadum (remove each piece after testing and always use a fresh piece). When the oil has reached the right temperature fry the poppadum one at a time, giving each side about five seconds. If you have room in the pan, cook them two at a time; doing this you will prevent the poppadum curling up. The idea is to keep them as flat as possible. Remove as soon as they

have reached their full size and stand on kitchen paper to drain. Ideally, poppadums should be served as fresh as possible but they should be thoroughly drained of oil.

GARAM MASALA

One of the other combined spices which has been much talked about by Indian cooks is garam masala. During my research for this book I have found that every cook I have talked to has his own special recipe for garam masala and so it seems an impossible task for me to recommend the right one. However, I will now give you a recipe for a garam masala that can be used universally throughout your curries, but by all means feel free to alter the ingredients to your taste. After all, if the Indian chefs can do it, there is no reason why you should not do it yourself.

25 g/1 oz cardamom seed
50 g/2 oz ground coriander
25 g/1 oz cloves
15 g/$\frac{1}{2}$ oz cumin seed or powder
15 g/$\frac{1}{2}$ oz mace
generous pinch freshly grated nutmeg

Combine all the ingredients in a shallow ovenproof dish and roast them in a moderate oven (180C, 350F, gas 4) for 20–30 minutes. Allow them to cool and then grind in a coffee grinder or a mortar and pestle. Store the spices in an airtight bottle.

Note When storing spices, it cannot be too highly stressed that the secret of good flavour is to keep your spices in tip-top condition. You can only do this by using airtight containers for all spices.

Fish & Shellfish

Spicy fish curries can be quite light as well as delicious and economical. This selection of recipes offers ideas for the more expensive prawns and crawfish as well as for plain cooked white fish. You will find that the cheaper types of fish, like coley, are often put to best use in spicy dishes where their strong flavour is balanced by the seasonings.

For a special, yet simple, meal serve spicy prawns cooked with spinach (Saag Prawn); garnished with lemon and served with fragrant Basmati rice this would make a deliciously light meal. If you find that you have leftover cooked fish then why not try the recipe for Mulchi Molee? This is a very basic recipe for cooked fish reheated in thick coconut milk which is spiced with chillies; a good dish to experiment with. Once you have tried some of these dishes you will find that keeping some fish fillets or prawns in the freezer is a good idea, because, with a few spices, they can be turned into an exotic meal.

STUFFED FISH

SERVES 4

1 (900-g 2-lb) halibut or 4 smaller
fish, for example plaice or sole
1 lemon
1 teaspoon salt
½ teaspoon paprika
25 g/1 oz blanched almonds
25 g/1 oz sultanas
50 g/2 oz ghee
1 large onion, sliced
½ teaspoon garam masala
175 g/6 oz mashed potatoes
1 teaspoon fresh root ginger, peeled
and chopped
1 small egg
2 green chillies, finely chopped
1½ teaspoons mint, chopped
vegetable oil
Garnish
tomato slices
lemon slices

Wash the fish and remove the eyes; wash out the insides. Do not remove the head. Cut the lemon in half and rub it all over the fish both inside and outside. Repeat this with some of the salt and the paprika. Leave for about 6 hours.

Fry the blanched almonds and the sultanas in the ghee and put them to one side. Fry the onions in the same ghee and then add the garam masala, the rest of the salt and the mashed potatoes. Left-overs are quite adequate for this. Allow to cool.

Blend the ginger, egg, fried almonds, sultanas, chillies and mint. Add to the onion and potato mixture and stuff the fish pressing it well into the body cavity.

Heat the vegetable oil in a frying pan until it is smoking and then add the fish and fry very quickly until it is crisp on the outside and thoroughly cooked through. Take care to keep as much of the stuffing in the fish as possible.

Serve whole, garnished with tomato and lemon slices, spooning any excess stuffing on to the plate with the fish.

Top: *Aviyal (page 44)*; below: *Stuffed Fish*

TANDOORI CRAWFISH

SERVES 4

In Britain the most common way to obtain uncooked crawfish is to buy them frozen. Sometimes they are known as 'large prawns' or 'lagousta'.

12 whole uncooked crawfish
300 ml/½ pint natural yogurt
150 ml/¼ pint vinegar
1 teaspoon salt
1 teaspoon ground black pepper
½ teaspoon paprika
½ teaspoon chilli powder
1 teaspoon garam masala
1 teaspoon ground fenugreek
red food colouring
25 g/1 oz fresh root ginger, peeled
and chopped
wedges of lemon to garnish

Prepare a marinade: put the yogurt and vinegar into a liquidiser with the salt, pepper, paprika, chilli powder, garam masala and fenugreek. Blend

Left: *Mulchi Molee;* right: *Saag Prawn (both recipes opposite)*

until a smooth sauce is obtained. Red colouring should be added until the sauce is quite red.

Put the prepared marinade to one side and turn your attention to the crawfish. The heads are sometimes removed by the fishmonger and the body left with six legs dangling from the shell. If the head has been left on, simply cut this off with a sharp knife. Now pull off the legs and the central section of the shell by inserting your thumb under the shell. The tail part of the shell should now pull off along with the front part of the shell. Remove the sand track which runs along the back – it is essential to do this otherwise a completely new texture is given to the dish! Try not to break the crawfish up too much when doing this.

Pour the marinade over the shellfish, cover and marinate for 2 days in the refrigerator.

The traditional way of cooking this is in a tandoor on skewers but you can use an ordinary charcoal barbecue or a grill. As with any tandoori cooking, the emphasis must be on thorough cooking so it is important not to have the heat too high. Thread the crawfish on to metal skewers and grill, turning once, until cooked – about 10 minutes. Serve immediately garnished with lemon.

MUCHLI MOLEE
SERVES 4

Molee is the name given to dishes cooked with a basis of thick coconut milk. Molee dishes are usually found in the south and east of India and on the Sri Lankan coast. In general, cooked fish is used to prepare a molee dish so any left-over fish pie can be used. The only difficult ingredient needed is the coconut milk which can be bought from an Indian supplier or can be made by grating out the inside of a fresh coconut and pouring about 300 ml/$\frac{1}{2}$ pint of boiling water on to it. Set aside for 30 minutes and then strain to obtain a fairly thick coconut milk. In the following recipe frozen cod steaks may be used.

1 large onion, sliced
1 clove garlic, chopped
50 g/2 oz ghee
3 green chillies
1 teaspoon turmeric
600 ml/1 pint coconut milk
2 tablespoons vinegar
450 g/1 lb cooked fish
Garnish
coriander leaves
ground ginger

Fry the onion and garlic in the ghee in a deep frying pan.
  Remove the stalks of the chillies and cut lengthwise in halves. Fry these also, being careful not to allow any of the ingredients to brown.
  Add the turmeric and cook for 4 minutes on a very low heat.
  Add the coconut milk and vinegar and simmer gently for 10 minutes.
  Place the fish in the sauce and allow it to warm through thoroughly. If you are using whole fish it is advisable not to stir as they will quite easily break up.
  Garnish with coriander leaves and sprinkle with ground ginger.

SAAG PRAWN
SERVES 4

Saag prawn epitomises the way Indians have mastered the cooking of different flavours such as prawns and spinach which keep their own delicate taste.

450 g/1 lb frozen leaf spinach
50 g/2 oz ghee
1 large onion, sliced
2 cloves garlic, sliced
2 large tomatoes, sliced
$\frac{1}{2}$ teaspoon turmeric
$\frac{1}{2}$ teaspoon garam masala
$\frac{1}{2}$ teaspoon ground coriander
1 teaspoon chilli powder
$\frac{1}{2}$ teaspoon ground ginger
2 teaspoons sugar
2.5-cm/1-in piece cinnamon stick
$\frac{1}{2}$ teaspoon salt
450 g/1 lb prawns (shelled weight)
lemon to garnish (optional)

Chop the spinach coarsely.
  Melt the ghee in a frying pan and fry the onion and garlic for 5 minutes; add the spinach and fry for 10 minutes, turning constantly to ensure that none of it sticks to the pan.
  Add the tomatoes, turmeric, garam masala, coriander and chilli powder, ginger, sugar, cinnamon and salt. Simmer with a tightly-fitting lid for 15 minutes.
  Add the prawns and cook for 10 minutes or longer if fresh.
  Serve garnished with lemon if you like.

PRAWN PATHIA
SERVES 4

This dish is very popular in Indian restaurants in the West. The original dish used fresh prawns but most Indian restaurants have to use frozen prawns. However, using frozen prawns inflates the price so it is as well to be completely sure of what you are going to do in this dish before you attempt it. When preparing a spiced dish from any sea food which is noted for its delicate flavour, it is obviously essential to ensure that the spicing does not mar this fresh flavour. The following recipe for prawn pathia avoids this problem. Do not overcook the prawns.

2 large onions, sliced
225 g/8 oz ghee
50 g/2 oz desiccated coconut
1 teaspoon chilli powder
2 teaspoons paprika
2.5-cm/1-in piece cinnamon stick
2 bay leaves
1 teaspoon garam masala
2 teaspoons fenugreek
25 g/1 oz fresh root ginger, peeled
and chopped
100 g/4 oz tomato purée
300 ml/½ pint natural yogurt
450 g/1 lb prawns (shelled weight)

Fry the onions in the ghee until golden brown.

Add the desiccated coconut and cook until it also is golden brown. Use medium or coarse grade coconut and make sure when cooking that none of it sticks to the bottom of the pan.

Stir in the chilli powder, paprika, cinnamon, bay leaves, garam masala, fenugreek, and ginger, tomato purée and yogurt. Stir in well and if necessary add a little hot water to make the sauce the consistency of thickened yogurt.

When the mixture boils add the prawns immediately, turning down the heat, and simmer very slowly in a covered pot until the prawns are cooked. This could take anything from 15 to 30 minutes, depending on how thawed out the prawns were. If you find the sauce is too liquid remove the saucepan lid to allow some of the water to evaporate.

Note Because of the fenugreek in this dish you will notice that there is none of the fishy smell usually associated with prawn dishes.

JHINGHE KA TIKKA
SERVES 4

This recipe uses minced prawns and although it is an expensive way of using them this is a very interesting way of serving seafood. Fresh or frozen prawns may be used, the latter probably being both more economical and safer to use. This is one of those Indian dishes which one can serve with ordinary Western accompaniments like mashed potatoes and peas.

350 g/12 oz prawns (shelled weight)
2 cloves garlic
1 heaped tablespoon fresh root
ginger, chopped
1 green chilli
1 large onion
½ teaspoon turmeric
½ teaspoon ground black pepper
½ teaspoon salt
1 egg
breadcrumbs to coat
100 g/4 oz butter
Garnish
unshelled prawns, mint or parsley

Mince the prawns together with the garlic, ginger, chilli, onion, turmeric, black pepper and salt. Use the finest blade on the mincer or alternatively use a liquidiser but be careful not to reduce the mixture to a liquid pulp.

Mix in the egg and form into round croquettes approximately 5 cm/2 in. in diameter. Coat with the breadcrumbs, fry in the butter until golden brown on all sides, turning once. This should take about 6 or 7 minutes.

It is important to garnish this dish attractively. Use a few whole, unpeeled prawns or failing that, a few sprigs of mint or parsley.

Prawn Pathia with plain rice and bombay ducks (bottom right)

Chicken Dishes

Chicken, a once expensive food, is now very cheap to buy and available as large joints, drumsticks or boneless breasts. For a dinner party, a spicy chicken dish provides an excellent alternative to the more expensive cuts of meat.

In the following pages you will find many favourite recipes – Chicken Vindaloo, Tandoori Chicken, Chicken Biryani and Chicken Dhansak, for example. From the various regions of India, this chapter offers recipes which will appeal to all tastes. The notes on the recipes offer culinary advice as well as some interesting background information about certain dishes. Information on skinning and jointing a chicken is also given should you decide to prepare the bird by authentic methods.

For the true curry-lovers, many of the recipes in this chapter will be familiar from restaurant menus and a welcome addition to their kitchen repertoire. For cooks who are new to Indian cooking, there are some easily prepared, never-fail ideas.

CHICKEN VINDALOO

SERVES 4

Vindaloo is a way of cooking. The amount of chillies is not the most important aspect of this style of cooking, and the object is that you should be able to taste the nuances of flavour.

I 1.5-kg/3-lb oven-ready chicken
2 large onions, chopped
225 g/8 oz ghee
2 green chillies
25 g/1 oz fresh root ginger, peeled and chopped
3 cloves garlic, chopped
1½ teaspoons turmeric
1 teaspoon ground coriander
1 teaspoon garam masala
2 tablespoons vinegar
2 curry leaves (optional)
300 ml/½ pint water
1 teaspoon salt
50 g/2 oz desiccated coconut (optional)
2 tablespoons chopped coriander to garnish

Skin and joint the chicken. Fry the onions in the ghee together with the green chillies. When the onions are golden brown, add the ginger, garlic, turmeric, coriander and garam masala. Fry for a further 3 minutes.

Add the vinegar, curry leaves (if used) and the water, together with the chicken pieces. Cover and simmer for about 30 minutes. Test the chicken with a skewer: if you get a clear juice coming out, then it is done.

Remove the lid of the pot and boil rapidly until the liquid evaporates; add the salt and the coconut (if used), simmer for 15 minutes and serve. Garnish with the chopped coriander.

Chicken Vindaloo

TANDOORI CHICKEN

SERVES 4

The name tandoori comes from the Hindi word *tandoor*, which means a tall, cylindrical clay oven which was used originally in north India to cook meat dishes and bread. As in most tandoori meat dishes, the secret lies in the preparation especially in the marinating and rubbing-in process. This is a recipe which you can easily prepare at home: it utilises an oven-ready chicken and it is cooked in a conventional oven.

1 1.5-kg/3-lb oven-ready chicken
150 ml/¼ pint vinegar
600 ml/1 pint natural yogurt
2 large onions, quartered
4 cloves garlic
59 g/2 oz fresh root ginger, peeled
and roughly chopped
1 lemon, quartered
2 teaspoons garam masala
1 teaspoon chilli powder
1 teaspoon paprika
½ teaspoon yellow food colouring
1½ teaspoons salt
Garnish
1 lettuce heart, separated into leaves
1 tomato, cut into wedges
1 small onion, sliced and separated
into rings

Skin and quarter the chicken (see page 25) and make two 1-cm/½-inch deep cuts in each of the quarters. It is essential not to go too deep otherwise the chicken will break up during cooking.

Place the vinegar and a little of the yogurt in a liquidiser; switch the liquidiser on to its lowest speed and add pieces of onion, garlic and peeled ginger sparingly so that the liquidiser is not overloaded.

Add three-quarters of the lemon to the liquidiser; blend until a smooth sauce is obtained. Pour off a little of this liquid into a bowl and add the rest of the spices and food colouring but not the salt, mixing well to ensure that there are no lumps. Return the sauce to the liquidiser and blend for another 30 seconds, gradually adding the remaining yogurt.

If you have a food processor, then put the onion, garlic, ginger and lemon in first. Process these ingredients until fine, then add the vinegar and process to make a smooth sauce. Add the spices and food colouring, then process again at the same time slowly pouring in the yogurt.

Take the chicken quarters and rub well with the salt and the remaining quarters of lemon, ensuring that the juice gets right inside the cuts. This rubbing-in process makes it easier for the sauce to penetrate during the marinating process. Place the chicken pieces in a shallow baking tin or roasting tin, add the marinade, cover and chill for 24 to 48 hours.

Uncover the chicken, baste it with the marinade, then transfer it to a moderate oven (180C, 350F, gas 4). Cook for 1½ hours or until the pieces of chicken are tender and browned.

To serve, carefully lift the pieces of chicken out of the cooking juices. Arrange them on a heated serving platter or on warmed individual plates. Garnish with the small lettuce leaves, tucking them under the pieces of chicken. Add wedges of tomato and onion rings. Transfer the cooking liquid to a warmed serving bowl and serve it with the chicken.

Note If you like, buy chicken joints instead of jointing a whole bird. If you prefer serving boneless pieces, then use 4 large boned chicken breasts instead.

Tandoori Chicken with Parathas (page 60) and Poppadums

MEEN MOLI
SERVES 4

This is a Goanese dish, which uses either chicken or duck. If you are using duck be sure to reduce the amount of cooking oil used, as, coupled with the natural greasiness of the duck, the dish could become very oily.

1 1.5-kg/3-lb oven-ready chicken or
duck
vegetable oil
2 large onions, sliced
3 green chillies, sliced
3 cloves garlic, chopped
4 tablespoons garam masala
300 ml/½ pint vinegar
Garnish
tomato
lemon

Skin and joint the bird (see page 25) and fry the pieces in a little oil until golden brown. Put to one side.

Fry the onions, chillies and garlic for 5 minutes.

Add the garam masala to the vinegar to form a paste and pour into the pan. Fry for a further 8 minutes.

Add the meat and turn well, cover and cook on a low heat until tender.

Serve garnished with tomato and lemon.

CHICKEN BIRYANI
SERVES 4

There are many recipes for this dish; the following is one of the simplest and is the most economical way of using up left-overs as it only needs about 15 minutes (assuming you have the left-over chicken curry). The recipe can be adapted for any other left-over meat: for example, lamb biryani from roghan gosht, beef biryani from pasanda.

350 g/12 oz Basmati rice
350 g/12 oz left-over chicken
300 ml/½ pint left-over chicken curry
sauce
½ teaspoon orange food colouring
Garnish:
1 hard-boiled egg, sliced
2 tomatoes, quartered
1 green pepper, sliced

Chicken Biryani with Cucumber Raeta (page 50)

Cook the rice by boiling in twice its volume of water (see introduction). Drain and put in a hot oven to ensure that every grain is separate.

Heat the curry sauce in a frying pan until it boils and then add the chicken pieces. These should be cooked over high heat turning continuously to prevent sticking. After about 2 or 3 minutes the chicken should be well heated.

Add the cooked rice and the orange food colouring. Sauté the rice very quickly (not longer than 1 minute), until it has an homogeneous orange colour and the chicken is well mixed in. If the rice appears too dry, add a little more curry sauce or water.

Transfer to a hot oval platter and garnish with hard-boiled egg, tomato and green pepper.

Serve with Cucumber Raeta (see page 50).

DUM KA MURGH

SERVES 4

This is a Madrasee recipe not unlike one of the northern Indian chicken recipes except that the spices used are a lot hotter. The bird is rubbed with a spiced preparation rather than marinated in a spiced sauce. This particular method of cooking chicken is perhaps superior in taste even to the famed tandoori chicken.

1 1.5-kg/3-lb oven-ready chicken
450 g/1 lb onions, sliced
100 g/4 oz ghee
150 ml/¼ pint natural yogurt
2.5-cm/1-in piece cinnamon stick
½ teaspoon ground black pepper
2 cardamom seeds
½ teaspoon chilli powder
2 green chillies
15 g/½ oz fresh coriander
½ teaspoon ground ginger
2 teaspoons salt
2 teaspoons desiccated coconut

Skin and joint the chicken as described below.

Fry the onions in the ghee until golden brown.

Set aside about a quarter of the onion and place the remaining three quarters in a liquidiser together with the yogurt, cinnamon, pepper, cardamoms, chilli powder, chillies, coriander leaves, ground ginger, salt and coconut and blend for about 3 minutes.

Prick the chicken all over with a fork and rub the blended mixture well into the bird. This should take about 10 minutes. Leave for 4 hours.

Arrange the chicken in an ovenproof dish, pour the left-over ghee and the remaining quarter of the onion over the top of the chicken and cook in a moderate oven (180 C, 350 F, gas 4) for 1 hour until tender.

To Skin and Joint a Chicken

If using a frozen chicken, then make sure that it is thoroughly defrosted and remove the giblets from the body cavity. (These can be used to make stock, along with any other trimmings from the chicken.)

Before skinning the chicken use a strong pair of kitchen scissors to cut off the tips of the wings and leg joints. Place the chicken on a large chopping board. Put the breast uppermost and the body opening away from you. Pinch the skin on the top of the breast, snip it with the scissors, then cut it from back to front with a sharp knife.

Work on one side first, pulling the skin away from the flesh, turn the chicken over and pull the skin off the underside of the bird. Make slits as you go to ease the process when skinning the legs and wings. Skin the second side in the same way, then finally cut off the parson's nose. The skin can be used to flavour stock, but cut off any pieces of fat first or the result will be greasy.

For jointing the chicken you will need a good, sharp, heavy cook's knife and a pair of scissors. The chicken can be divided into four or six joints. To cut six joints, cut between the legs and the body of the chicken (between the breast and the joint) down behind the thigh. The thigh meat should be included as part of the leg portion.

Next remove the wing joints in the same way, cutting as near to the main body of the chicken as possible. Use a sturdy pair of kitchen scissors to snip any difficult pieces.

The chicken breast will be left: cut this in half along its length, then open the chicken out flat on a board. Split the opened out bird along the middle. For this you may have to use a wooden meat mallet to tap the knife. Discard any loose bone. The joints can be divided in half to make a total of 12 pieces.

If you want to split the chicken into four large joints, then start by cutting off the leg joints with the thighs. The wing joints are then cut with the breast. So each wing joint should include half the breast meat from the chicken. Alternatively, the breast meat can be slipped off the bone quite easily and separated from the wings to give two boneless fillets.

MURGH PALAK

SERVES 4

1 1.5-kg/3-lb oven-ready chicken
2 large onions, finely chopped
vegetable oil
1 clove garlic, crushed
1 large tomato, chopped
2 cloves
pinch of salt
½ teaspoon ground coriander
3 tablespoons milk
225 g/8 oz frozen leaf spinach
Garnish
fresh coriander
lemon

Skin and joint the chicken (see page 25).

Fry the onions finely in a little vegetable oil for 10 minutes.

Add the garlic and tomatoes together with the cloves, salt and coriander and fry for a further 5

Top: *Murgh Palak*; below: *Baigan Boortha* (page 46)

minutes. Add the milk and spinach. It is essential to keep turning the spinach to ensure that it is all cooked.

Add the chicken pieces and cover the pot with a tightly fitting lid. Cook on a very low heat for about 1½ hours or until the chicken is tender.

Garnish with coriander leaves and lemon.

CHICKEN CURRY

SERVES 4

1 1.75-kg/4-lb boiling fowl
350 g/12 oz ghee
675 g/1½ lb onions, sliced
100 g/4 oz fresh root ginger, peeled
7 or 8 cloves garlic
600 ml/1 pint water
2 teaspoons turmeric
2 teaspoons garam masala
3 teaspoons salt
3 teaspoons ground cumin
½ teaspoon ground black pepper
1 teaspoon chilli powder
10 cardamom seeds
10 cloves
4 bay leaves
5 cinnamon sticks
300 ml/½ pint natural yogurt

Skin and joint the chicken (see page 25).

Use a large heavy-based saucepan; melt the ghee, and add half the onions.

While they are frying on a gentle heat, blend the ginger, garlic and the rest of the onions with the water. Add this to the onions when they are golden brown; stir on a low heat for 10 minutes.

Add the turmeric, garam masala, salt, cumin, pepper, chilli powder, cardamom seeds, cloves, bay leaves, and cinnamon and stir for a further 10 minutes.

Add the chicken pieces and the yogurt. Cover the pan and cook on a low heat for 3 hours. The spices will have permeated the meat to the bone, and the flesh will fall away at a touch when properly done.

Serve with rice.

HYDERABAD CHICKEN CURRY
SERVES 4

This chicken curry differs from the conventional one in that it makes use of sliced coconut to give it a flavour and texture peculiar to the Deccan area of India. It is somewhat sweeter than usual with the tomato purée. When the chicken is finally added, it should be cooked gently until tender. It is always better to let this type of curry cook for longer if necessary and thereby ensure a tender, well-cooked dish.

1 large onion, sliced
50 g/2 oz ghee
2 cloves garlic, sliced
2 cardamom seeds
2 cloves
5-cm/2-in piece cinnamon stick
2 teaspoons garam masala
1 teaspoon chilli powder
1 1.5-kg/3-lb oven-ready chicken
100 g/4 oz tomato purée
300 ml/½ pint water
½ coconut
1 lemon to garnish

Fry the onion for 2 or 3 minutes in the ghee, together with the garlic, cardamoms, cloves, cinnamon, garam masala and chilli powder. Stir well for 5 minutes. Leave to simmer for 5 to 10 minutes on a low heat.

Meanwhile, skin and joint the chicken (see page 25). Add together with the tomato purée. Increase the heat and turn the chicken well.

Turn the heat down and add the hot water.

Scrape out the inside of the coconut in large chunks and slice thinly. Add to the pot and cover closely; simmer for 1 hour or until the chicken is tender.

Just before serving sprinkle shredded whole lemon over the top.

CHICKEN DHANSAK
SERVES 4

This is a famous Parsee Indian dish which has become well known throughout the West as the chicken dish with lentils. The word 'dhansak' means wealthy, and thus a dhansak is a very special dish. However, in the Western world it is not quite so special as it can be made using fatty meat from the cheaper cuts, the best being the breast of lamb. To make a good dhansak is rather complicated, and as there are numerous recipes, I have tried to select one which is clear and easy to follow.

175 g/6 oz chenna dal
175 g/6 oz moong dal
900 ml/1½ pints water
2 large onions, sliced
175 g/6 oz ghee
2 cloves
3 cloves garlic, sliced
1 teaspoon ground ginger
1 teaspoon garam masala
675 g/1½ lb chicken joints
1 medium aubergine
2 large tomatoes
225 g/8 oz frozen spinach
2 teaspoons salt

Wash the dals well and mix together. Place both in a large saucepan and cover with the water. Boil gently for 15 minutes.

Meanwhile, fry the onions in a heavy-based pan in the ghee for 5 minutes; add the cloves, garlic, ginger and garam masala.

Sauté the thawed chicken joints for 1 minute in the same pot on a very high heat, remove, drain and keep on one side.

Cut the aubergine and tomatoes into 2.5-cm/1-in pieces and add with the spinach to the ghee. Cook for 10 minutes.

The lentils should by now be quite well cooked; mash them with their water to form a sauce and pour in the vegetables from the other saucepan. Stir in well until you have a thick stew.

Add the sautéed chicken joints and salt, cover with a lid and cook on a low heat until the chicken falls off the bone easily.

Meat Dishes

This chapter includes a broad range of dishes for beef, lamb and pork, including ideas for mince and liver. Pork is not commonly eaten in India (in fact it is strictly forbidden for many Indians) but when it is cooked it is used in particularly tasty dishes.

Again, favourite recipes are here – Beef Curry, Roghan Gosht and Lamb Korma for example. For these who like a good kick in their spiced dishes, there is also a recipe for Mutton Madras.

Minced beef and lamb are about the cheapest cuts of meat which are available (many supermarkets now offer minced lamb) and they can be turned into quite mouth-watering, authentic Indian meals. If you cannot obtain minced lamb, then ask your butcher to mince trimmed shoulder of lamb, or mince it yourself.

Remember, too, when planning summer meals to try cooking some of these kebabs on a barbecue. The air will be filled with the most appetising of aromas, and appetites will be aroused to the full.

CALCUTTA BEEF CURRY

SERVES 4

(Illustrated on page 30)

The following recipe is a typical dish of Calcutta, being basically a curry prepared with a thin gravy which has a high proportion of ghee in it. It is a very useful way of using up any of the poorer quality cuts of meat such as shin of beef.

450 g / 1 lb boneless beef
600 ml / 1 pint water
2 teaspoons ground coriander
½ teaspoon turmeric
½ teaspoon ground cumin
1 tablespoon chilli powder
½ teaspoon ground black pepper
2 teaspoons salt
1 teaspoon ground ginger
little milk to mix
1 large onion, sliced
1 clove garlic, sliced
25 g / 1 oz ghee
fresh coriander or parsley to garnish

Cut any fat off the beef and cut into 3.5-cm/1½-in chunks; simmer in the lightly salted water until tender.

Mix together the coriander, turmeric, cumin, chilli powder, pepper, salt and ginger to make a paste, using a little milk.

Fry the onion and garlic in the ghee until golden brown. Add the paste and fry for a further 3 minutes.

Add the meat together with half the water in which it has been boiling. Bring to the boil and simmer for 15 minutes, adding some of the remaining water if the gravy appears too thick.

Serve garnished with a little chopped green coriander or parsley.

Roghan Gosht (page 30) with Palao Rice (page 57)

ROGHAN GOSHT

SERVES 4

(Illustrated on previous page)

The prowess of a north Indian cook is often judged by her ability to prepare roghan gosht. Consequently, there exist any number of recipes for this dish and some cooks insist on lengthy lists of ingredients sometimes over twenty items long. But the secret of roghan gosht lies not so much in the number of ingredients as in the way they are put together.

450 g/1 lb lean boneless lamb
1½ teaspoons salt
300 ml/½ pint natural yogurt
2 large onions
225 g/8 oz ghee
50 g/2 oz fresh root ginger, peeled and chopped
4 cloves garlic
150 ml/¼ pint water
½ teaspoon ground black pepper
2 teaspoons paprika
1 teaspoon ground cumin
50 g/2 oz tomato purée

Cut the meat into 2.5-cm/1-in cubes, then add the salt to the yogurt and rub well into the meat. Cover and leave in the refrigerator for 24 hours.

Slice the onions and fry in the ghee until golden brown. Use a large heavy-based saucepan for both the frying and the main cooking. Put the ginger and garlic in a liquidiser with the water and blend until smooth. Add to the onions. Simmer for 10 minutes.

Add the rest of the spices, stir well and simmer for 10 minutes. Add tomato purée and stir for 5 minutes. Then add the meat with the marinade, cover and cook gently for 1¼ hours or until the meat is tender.

PASANDA

SERVES 4

This dish is to be found more in Pakistan than in India as of course, Hindus do not eat beef. It is very similar to roghan gosht in its preparation but as the quality of beef is usually inferior to that of lamb, the authentic recipe calls for a period of marination. This can last up to 6 days but a relatively tender cut of meat needs only 24 hours.

Top: *Calcutta Beef Curry;* below: *Matar Panir* (page 46)

450 g/1 lb lean boneless beef
1½ teaspoon salt
300 ml/½ pint natural yogurt
2 large onions, chopped
225 g/8 oz ghee
50 g/2 oz fresh root ginger, peeled and chopped
4 cloves garlic, chopped
2 teaspoons ground coriander
1 teaspoon garam masala
½ teaspoon chilli powder
2 teaspoons paprika
½ teaspoon ground cumin
2 teaspoons turmeric

Cut the beef into 1-cm/½-in thick slices. Tenderise the meat with either a tenderising machine or a mallet.

Rub the salt into the meat and marinate it in the yogurt for 24 hours or longer.

In a large, heavy pot fry the onions until golden brown in the ghee. Add the ginger and garlic with the rest of the spices. Stir well.

Add the meat with the yogurt and cook for 45 minutes to 1¼ hours, until tender.

TIKKA KEBAB
SERVES 4

There is nothing very complicated about preparing this dish, but the result is exquisite. Essentially the dish consists of marinated cubes of lean meat gently barbecued. Tikka kebab is at its best when cooked over a charcoal fire and thus is very good for an open air barbecue. However, quite reasonable results can be obtained by cooking it under a grill. The secret is in the preparation. In India goat meat is usually used but of course lamb will give perfectly acceptable results.

1 medium onion, chopped
3 tablespoons vegetable oil
450 g/1 lb lean boneless lamb
½ lemon
2 cloves garlic
25 g/1 oz fresh root ginger, peeled and chopped
1 teaspoon garam masala
1 teaspoon paprika
1 teaspoon salt
3 tablespoons vinegar
300 ml/½ pint natural yogurt
Garnish
onion rings
wedges of lemon

Add the onion to the oil.

Cut the meat into 2.5-cm/1-in cubes, trimming away any excess fat.

Rub the lemon over the meat. It is best to use a shallow baking tin for this. Rub the oil and onion mixture over the meat. It is important to get to grips with the meat and knead it well.

Blend the remaining ingredients in a liquidiser into a smooth mixture.

Add this mixture to the meat and mix in well. The cubes of meat should be covered by the liquid. Marinate in a cool place.

Thread about four cubes onto a normal sized skewer and place over the charcoal or under the grill. Cook slowly to ensure even cooking, turning occasionally.

Serve immediately when the outside starts to go dark brown. Tikka kebab is usually eaten with bread such as parathas.

Garnish with onion rings and wedges of lemon.

Note This dish is better the longer the meat is marinated. For very lean and tender meat 24 hours should be sufficient, but there is nothing wrong with leaving it up to a week in a cool place.

LAMB KORMA
SERVES 4

The most popular korma is made with lamb. It has an interesting combination of nuts and meat cooked in a sauce that seems to complement the flavours of both. The secret of korma is the use of saffron; although it may seem very expensive it is the most essential part of this dish.

450 g/1 lb lean boneless leg or shoulder of lamb
½ teaspoon saffron
3–4 tablespoons boiling water
50 g/2 oz unsalted cashew nuts
3 green chillies
25 g/1 oz fresh root ginger, peeled and chopped
2.5 cm/1-in piece cinnamon stick
½ teaspoon cardamom seeds
6 cloves
3 cloves garlic
2 teaspoons ground coriander
½ teaspoon cumin seeds
300 ml/½ pint water
100 g/4 oz ghee
1 large onion, sliced
1 teaspoon salt
300 ml/½ pint natural yogurt
1 tablespoon fresh coriander, chopped
2 teaspoons lemon juice
fresh coriander to garnish

Cut any fat off the lamb and cut into 2.5-cm/1-in cubes. Place the saffron in a bowl and pour in 3 or 4 tablespoons boiling water. Infuse for 10 minutes.

Place the cashew nuts, chillies, ginger, cinnamon, cardamoms, cloves, garlic, coriander and cumin seeds in a liquidiser together with the water and blend for 2 minutes to a smooth purée.

Heat the ghee until very hot (a good test of this is when the water is flicked into it splutters instantly). Fry the onion in the ghee until golden brown. Stir in the salt and the blended spices and the yogurt. Cook gently for 5 minutes stirring occasionally.

Add the lamb pieces turning to ensure that they are well coated. Now add the saffron together with the water in which it has been soaking and reduce the heat to very low. Cook for 20 minutes in a covered pan, stirring occasionally.

Add the fresh coriander and cook for another 10 minutes, or until the lamb is tender. Serve with lemon juice, garnished with coriander.

MUTTON DOPIAZAH
SERVES 4

A dopiazah is any dish which contains a large proportion of onions. How much is entirely up to the individual cook. It has an interesting sweet, hot taste which varies according to the amount of onions used. The essential requirement is that some of the onion should be fried at the beginning and some added raw when the mutton has been half cooked. One can also use beef or chicken.

450 g/1 lb onions, sliced
175 g/6 oz ghee
450 g/1 lb mutton (or shoulder of lamb)
1 teaspoon chilli powder
300 ml/½ pint natural yogurt
½ teaspoon ground ginger
1 teaspoon salt
2 cloves garlic, crushed
4 cardamom seeds
1 teaspoon garam masala
½ teaspoon cumin seeds

Fry half of the onions in the ghee until golden brown. Remove from the ghee and set to one side.

Cut the mutton into 2.5-cm/1-in cubes and sauté in the ghee until sealed on both sides. Remove the meat and set aside.

Add the chilli powder and remaining onions along with the yogurt, ginger and salt. Cook for 2 minutes and add the meat. Cover and simmer for 10 minutes.

Add the garlic to the saucepan (it may be necessary to add some water to prevent the mixture from becoming too dry), then add the browned onions, cardamoms, garam masala and cumin. Cover and simmer for 30 minutes.

Top right: *Muttom Madras (page 34)*; left: *Tali Kaleja (page 34)*

MUTTON MADRAS

SERVES 4

(Illustrated on previous page)

The amounts given here are sufficient to make a hot curry. The more intrepid may choose to add even more chilli.

450 g/1 lb mutton
50 g/2 oz ghee
1 large onion, sliced
2 teaspoons garam masala
2 teaspoons chilli powder
75 g/3 oz tomato purée
3 cardamom seeds, crushed
1 teaspoon salt
juice of ½ lemon

Cut any fat from the mutton and cut into 2.5-cm/1-in cubes; fry gently in the ghee to seal.

Remove the meat and fry the onion with the garam masala and chilli powder for 4 minutes.

Add the meat together with the tomato purée and the cardamoms. Stir well and cover the pan with a close-fitting lid. Simmer gently for about 30 minutes, stirring occasionally. Add water if the curry appears to be dry, but the sauce should be quite thick.

Add the salt and the lemon juice. Simmer very slowly for another 15 minutes until the meat is tender. Serve with plain rice.

TALI KALEJA

SERVES 4

(Illustrated on previous page)

Kaleja is the Indian name for liver, and tali means fried. The method of cooking liver here brings out the flavour of the liver without allowing it to become too dry.

1 small onion, sliced
mustard oil for cooking
½ teaspoon turmeric
½ teaspoon chilli powder
½ teaspoon ground black pepper
½ teaspoon ground ginger
½ teaspoon salt
225 g/½ lb liver
1 clove garlic, chopped
Garnish
tomatoes
chopped fresh coriander

Fry the onion in the mustard oil using a heavy-based frying pan.

Mix the turmeric, chilli powder, pepper and ginger with the salt and make this into a paste with a little water.

Cut the liver into 5-mm/¼-in thick slices and wash well; pat dry and rub the spice paste into each slice.

Add together with the garlic to the pan, cover and cook for 10 minutes until the liver is tender.

Serve garnished with chopped tomatoes and a little chopped coriander.

KEEMA PIMENTO

SERVES 4

(Illustrated on page 41)

The green pepper, is among the few exotic vegetables that are readily available at most greengrocers. However, although the green pepper's fate is usually to garnish an otherwise tired green salad, there are other uses for this delicious vegetable, and I consider the following recipe for keema pimento does it more than justice.

450 g/1 lb green peppers
vegetable oil
450 g/1 lb onions, sliced
2 teaspoons salt
2 teaspoons ground black pepper
½ teaspoon ground cumin
2 teaspoons garam masala
pinch of ground cinnamon
1½ teaspoons chilli powder
1.5 kg/3 lb raw minced meat
Garnish
green pepper rings
tomatoes

Cut the green peppers into 5-mm/¼-in strips, discarding all the seeds, the white centre and the green stalk. Heat the oil in a heavy pan and sauté the strips for about a minute. Transfer to a dish and place in a warm oven.

Add the onions to the oil and fry until golden brown. Add the salt, black pepper, cumin, garam masala, cinnamon and chilli powder and stir for 2 minutes.

Add the minced meat and cook gently for about 20 minutes until well done, stirring to make sure that none sticks to the bottom of the pan.

Add the green peppers and stir again over a very low heat, for a further 10 minutes.

Serve garnished with rings of green pepper and tomato.

KOFTA CURRY

SERVES 4

This dish is nearly always found at Indian parties, notably wedding feasts, because it is cheap to produce and it goes well with the other great 'filler up' – rice. If you have never cooked Indian food before, this is probably the best dish to start with.

450 g/1 lb raw minced meat
450 g/1 lb onions
6 cloves garlic
25 g/1 oz parsley
1 egg
oil for deep frying
100 g/4 oz ghee
2 teaspoons salt
1 teaspoon chilli powder
1 teaspoon ground black pepper
1 teaspoon ground cumin
2 teaspoons garam masala
2 teaspoons paprika
1 teaspoon turmeric
50 g/2 oz fresh root ginger, peeled and chopped
300 ml/½ pint natural yogurt

Clockwise from top: _Palao rice (page 57), Kofta Curry and Baigan Tamatar (page 38)_

Mince the meat again through a mincer along with half the onions, three cloves of garlic and the parsley.

Add the egg to the resulting mixture and mix well with the hands. Form into 2.5-cm/1-in diameter balls. Deep-fry the balls for 2 minutes in hot oil.

Slice the remaining onions and fry in the ghee until golden brown. Add the spices and stir well for 10 minutes.

Add the meat balls and simmer for 30 minutes turning the balls frequently to ensure that they do not stick to the bottom of the pot.

Finally add the yogurt and simmer for a further 30 minutes, stirring well.

SEEKH KEBAB

SERVES 4

The word _seekh_ in Hindi means a skewer, and 'seekh kebab' is simply a kebab on a skewer. This skewer of kebab was originally cooked in the tandoor and a lot of the essential flavour of the seekh kebab comes from the charcoal smoke of the fire. The best Western compromise is a charcoal barbecue.

450 g/1 lb raw minced lamb
2 medium onions
2 tablespoons breadcrumbs
50 g/2 oz fresh coriander
½ teaspoon salt
1 teaspoon garam masala
1 tablespoon green pepper, finely chopped
1 tablespoon lemon juice
Garnish
lettuce
cucumber

Mince the meat again through a mincer with the onions, breadcrumbs, coriander, salt, garam masala and green pepper.

Add the lemon juice to the mixture and form into balls about 5 cm/2 in. in diameter. Push these on to the skewer and gradually mould them into sausage shapes along the metal.

Cook the kebabs gently over a low heat with a barbecue or grill, or in a moderate oven (180C, 350F, gas 4) for 15 to 20 minutes. When the meat comes off the skewer cleanly, the kebab is cooked right through. Serve on a bed of lettuce and cucumber.

Note The idea behind the seekh kebab is to spice the meat in such a way that it involves no pre-cooking of a spiced sauce. This is done by passing the already minced meat through a mincer with the various spices. The skewers used in India are made of iron or steel and are approximately 90 cm/3 ft long and 9 mm/⅜ in. in diameter. The seekh kebab is first formed into a ball about 5 cm/2 in. in diameter and then moulded into a sausage-shape on the skewers. When re-using the skewers it is essential to make sure that they are clean otherwise you will have problems removing the next set of kebabs.

Top: _Pork Vindaloo_; below: _Seekh Kebab_

PORK VINDALOO

SERVES 4

Pork is strictly forbidden for many Indians. Pigs are hardly ever bred as such and a lot of the pork that is eaten is of the _shikar_ type – the wild boar. Even for those Indians to whom it is not strictly forbidden, the eating of pork is not encouraged, since the climatic conditions are not very favourable. None-theless, the few Indians who do eat pork have developed some very exotic and tasty ways of cooking it.

2 large onions, sliced
8 cloves garlic, sliced
175 g/6 oz ghee
675 g/1½ lb lean boneless pork
½ teaspoon paprika
½ teaspoon turmeric
1 teaspoon fenugreek seeds
25 g/1 oz fresh root ginger, peeled and chopped
2 green chillies
1 teaspoon salt
150 ml/¼ pint water
50 g/2 oz tamarind
1½ teaspoons garam masala
2 bay leaves
6 cardamoms
3 cloves
fresh coriander leaves to garnish

Fry the onions and garlic in the ghee. Cut any fat from the pork and cut into 2.5-cm/1-in cubes and fry in a little ghee to seal the juices.

Remove the pot from the heat and add the paprika, turmeric, fenugreek, ginger, chillies and salt. Add the water and cook gently for about 20 or 30 minutes in a covered pot until the meat is tender.

Soak the tamarind for 30 minutes to form a pulp.

Uncover the pot and bring to the boil and evaporate nearly all the water. Add the rest of the spices and the tamarind pulp and cook on a very low heat for approximately 30 minutes. Serve garnished with coriander.

Vegetable Dishes

Exotic vegetables of all types are now sold in many supermarkets and greengrocers, so it makes sense to try some new and interesting recipes which use them.

Aubergines, okra and spinach are used in a variety of Indian recipes. With onions, spices, chillies and tomatoes they can be turned into a variety of dishes which are both subtle and aromatic.

Also included are recipes for marrows, cauliflower, cabbage, yams and lentils – all ingredients which are easily available. Serve these vegetables as accompaniments for a fish, poultry or meat dish. Alternatively, serve several vegetable dishes with some rice and lentils, or perhaps some bread and a raeta to make a superb vegetarian meal.

If, on the other hand, you want to make a light lunch or supper, then serve a spicy aubergine dish with some freshly cooked Indian bread – delicious!

BAIGAN TAMATAR

SERVES 4

(Illustrated on page 35)

With the exception of ladies' fingers (okra), baigan tamatar is probably the most popular dish available in the tandoori-style restaurants. It typifies the blandness of the northern Indian cuisine and you actually know what you are eating.

2 medium onions, chopped
225 g/8 oz ghee
1 small clove garlic, chopped
½ teaspoon chilli powder
1 bay leaf
2.5-cm/1-in piece of cinnamon stick
1½ teaspoons salt
½ teaspoon ground black pepper
little water
450 g/1 lb tomatoes, peeled and quartered
450 g/1 lb aubergines, cubed
2 tablespoons tomato purée

Fry the onions in the ghee until golden brown. Add the garlic, chilli powder, bay leaf, cinnamon, salt and black pepper with a little water. Bring to the boil, stirring constantly.

Add the tomatoes and continue to boil for 5 minutes.

Add the aubergines to the pot with the tomato purée. Simmer for 30 minutes until the aubergines are tender but do not overcook otherwise they will disintegrate.

Note Always choose firm aubergines which at the height of the season should be almost black in colour. Tinned aubergines are virtually useless for this dish. The tomatoes may, however, be as ripe as you like, provided that they are still firm and the skins are not broken.

BHINDI BHAJI

SERVES 4

Bhindi or ladies' fingers or okra is the vegetable that everybody associates with Indian cooking. Dishes to be shunned when eating in an Indian restaurant are those that come with the bhindi whole since these have undoubtedly been made from canned bhindi, and canning never successfully preserves the bhindi's essential flavour. If the bhindi comes in a chopped form it is fresh. The essence of cooking bhindi is that you should taste the vegetable and not anything else.

2 large onions
175 g/6 oz ghee
4 cloves garlic
pinch of black pepper
pinch of salt
2 teaspoons ground coriander
$\frac{1}{2}$ teaspoon turmeric
450 g/1 lb fresh bhindi
100 g/4 oz canned tomatoes
1 teaspoon fresh mint, chopped
$\frac{1}{2}$ teaspoon garam masala
fresh mint to garnish (optional)

Bhindi Bhaji

Slice one onion and fry in the ghee in a heavy-based pan.

Blend the remaining onion and the garlic in a liquidiser with the black pepper, salt, coriander and turmeric. Add this mixture to the onions and cook on a medium heat for 5 minutes.

Meanwhile, prepare the bhindi. Wash thoroughly and top and tail each of the ladies' fingers. Chop them into 1-cm/$\frac{1}{2}$-in pieces.

Add the bhindi to the spices. Stir carefully, so that they are not crushed or mashed. Cover the pan with a lid and cook over a very low heat for about 20 minutes.

Add the tomatoes, the mint and the garam masala. The bhindi will be quite soft by now so it is even more important to be careful when stirring in these ingredients. Simmer for 15 minutes.

Serve garnished with fresh mint if you like.

SAAG ALOO
SERVES 4

Most Western people with the exception of the Americans, have an aversion to spinach. Whilst they will agree that it is good for the constitution, they will usually on no account touch it themselves. This is a great shame because, like cabbage, spinach when properly cooked is a very tasty vegetable. Saag aloo is one of the few dishes which really brings out the fresh taste of spinach. If you can bring yourself to throw tradition to the winds I am sure that you will find it is a very worthwhile dish.

2 large onions, sliced
100 g/4 oz ghee
½ teaspoon coriander seeds
½ teaspoon cumin seeds
½ teaspoon chilli powder
½ teaspoon ground coriander
900 g/2 lb fresh spinach or 450 g/1 lb frozen spinach
450 g/1 lb potatoes, peeled and cubed
½ teaspoon salt
2 teaspoons ground fenugreek
2 green chillies (optional)
100 g/4 oz canned tomatoes
50 g/2 oz fresh root ginger, peeled and thinly sliced

Fry half the onions in the ghee in a heavy-based saucepan until golden brown. Then add the coriander and cumin seeds and cook for 1 minute.

Blend the rest of the onions and the chilli powder together with the ground coriander in a liquidiser. Stir in the purée into the onions. Cook for 5 minutes.

Wash the spinach and chop it into small pieces. Cook for 10 minutes until it is tender.

Parboil the cubed potatoes for 5 to 8 minutes in slightly salted water.

Drain the potatoes and add, with the spinach, salt, fenugreek and chillies (if used) to the main pot. Stir in well and cook on a very low heat for about 10 minutes, turning occasionally.

Add the tomatoes and ginger. Cover and simmer for 10 minutes. Serve immediately.

BAIGAN MASALEWALA
SERVES 4

The following recipe is rather peculiar for an Indian dish in that it makes use of the technique of roasting, a practice that is not always easy in India and Pakistan due to the lack of suitable ovens. This dish can also be fried but baking retains a lot of the original flavour of the aubergines. Aubergines vary a great deal in size and shape. The most readily available are the long variety: these are most suitable for making thin slices for pakoras (see page 58). However, they also come in shorter, squat shapes which are the type you need for this dish.

4 aubergines (round variety)
1 teaspoon salt
½ teaspoon ground white pepper
1 large onion, chopped
100 g/4 oz ghee
100 g/4 oz peas
100 g/4 oz fresh carrots, diced or well drained canned carrots
225 g/8 oz tomatoes, peeled and chopped
½ teaspoon paprika
1 teaspoon fresh root ginger, finely chopped or ½ teaspoon ground ginger
mint or parsley to garnish

Wash the aubergines and remove the thick leafy sepals at the top of each one. Parboil in slightly salted water for about 10 minutes.

Cut each one in half and scoop out the pulp leaving about 1 cm/½ in all the way around. Season the cases with a pinch of the salt and pepper.

In a heavy-based pan fry the onions lightly in the ghee, add the peas (these may be fresh, dried, or frozen but not canned), and the carrots.

Chop the aubergine pulp and add it to the frying pan with the tomatoes. Cook gently until all the vegetables are tender.

Add the paprika, the rest of the salt and the ginger. Stir for 2 minutes

Arrange the aubergine halves in a baking tray and fill each case with the fried pulp. Place the tray in a moderate oven (180 C, 350 F, gas 4) and bake for about 20 minutes, until golden brown.

Serve garnished with mint or parsley.

Top: *Keema Pimento (page 34)*; below: *Baigan Masalewala*

GOODHI BHAJI

SERVES 4

Marrows are freely available in most Western countries and are very easy to grow. This recipe, a typically vegetarian one, makes use of only young marrows which should never be more than about 15–18 cm/6–7 in. in length. The Indian method of spicing brings out the true flavour of the marrow.

900 g/2 lb young marrow or
courgettes
vegetable oil
1½ teaspoons mustard seeds
2 medium onions, sliced
2 tomatoes, sliced
1½ teaspoons garam masala
½ teaspoon turmeric
1 teaspoon chilli powder
1 teaspoon ground black pepper
½ teaspoon salt
75 g/3 oz desiccated coconut
wedges of lemon to garnish

Peel the marrow or courgettes, cut lengthways and scoop out all the seeds. Dice into 2.5-cm/1-in cubes.

Heat a little of the vegetable oil until smoking; add the mustard seeds and fry until they begin to splutter. Add a little more of the vegetable oil and the onions. Fry until golden brown.

Add the tomatoes together with the garam masala, turmeric, chilli powder, and black pepper, and fry gently on a low heat for 5 or 6 minutes.

Rub the marrow with the salt and the desiccated coconut. Add to the pot and simmer covered for about 15 minutes. Serve with wedges of lemon.

ONION PAKORA

SERVES 4

(Illustrated on page 45)
Onion pakoras make a popular hors d'oeuvre or starter. They are very simple to make using the pakora recipe (see page 58). The recipe below is for preparing the onion before use.

2 large onions
600 ml/1 pint natural yogurt
1 tablespoon fresh root ginger,
peeled and chopped
1 clove garlic
1 teaspoon chilli powder
½ lemon
1 teaspoon salt
vegetable oil
1 quantity Pakora Batter (page 58)
fresh coriander leaves to garnish

Cut the onions crossways to form rings.

Place all the other ingredients with the exception of the oil and batter in a liquidiser and blend to a thin pulp. Marinate the onion rings in this mixture overnight.

Prepare the batter according to the recipe instructions. Lift the onion rings from the marinade and drain well. Heat the oil for deep frying to 190C/375F. To cook, dip each ring into the pakora batter and fry individually in the hot fat until golden. You will find this method imparts far more flavour to the otherwise conventional onion pakora. Drain on absorbent kitchen paper and serve hot, garnished with fresh coriander leaves.

Tarka Dal (overleaf) with plain rice

TARKA DAL

SERVES 4

(Illustrated on page 42)

Dal forms part of the staple diet of a very large percentage of the Indian population. It is in essence very simple in its preparation. In Great Britain most people are only familiar with lentils whilst in America chick-peas as well-known, but in addition to these two there is a whole range of grams and pulses which the Indians make into a delicious, thick soup-like sauce to accompany their otherwise plain rice. The following recipe makes use of the ordinary, easily available, red split lentils.

450 g / 1 lb lentils
1.15 litres / 2 pints water
1 teaspoon salt
1 teaspoon turmeric
1 medium onion
3 cloves garlic
2 chillies
Garnish
garlic
½ teaspoon cumin seeds
little vegetable oil

Wash the dal in a large pot, running the cold tap on it continuously while you stir it. Keep a good look out for the odd small stone that may have settled and not been washed away.

Place the dal in a saucepan and cover with the water. Bring to the boil and add the salt, turmeric and onion and 2 cloves of the garlic along with the chillies. Cover and simmer for about 20 minutes until cooked. When cooked the dal should be yellow in colour and have the consistency of sloppy porridge.

The secret of tarka dal lies in the serving. It should be served piping hot garnished with cumin seeds and slices of quick-fried garlic.

AVIYAL

SERVES 4

(Illustrated on page 15)

Aviyal is the name given to any southern Indian vegetable dish which includes a mixture of many vegetables and seeds. Exotic fruits, seeds and vegetables like jackfruit, drumsticks, bitter gourds, green coconut and mango are very difficult to obtain in the West, unless canned which is useless for good vegetable cooking. The following recipe utilises only those freely available vegetables such as carrots, broccoli and green beans. The recipe can be used as the basis for making many vegetable dishes. So, after making this one, try adding different vegetables – the only things you must be sure of are that they are cooked, and that the spices do not mask the flavour.

225 g / 8 oz desiccated coconut
300 ml / ½ pint water
100 g / 4 oz ghee
25 g / 1 oz fresh root ginger, peeled and chopped
3 cloves garlic, chopped
½ teaspoon mustard seeds
1 large onion, chopped
2 teaspoons ground coriander
3 teaspoons garam masala
1 teaspoon turmeric
2 teaspoons salt
225 g / 8 oz broccoli or kale
2 green peppers
175 g / 6 oz carrots
100 g / 4 oz runner beans
1 green chilli
100 g / 4 oz fresh coriander to garnish

Blend the coconut and water together in a liquidiser to produce a smooth purée.

Heat the ghee in a heavy-based saucepan and add the ginger, garlic, and mustard seeds and fry for about 1 minute. Add the onion and fry until golden brown, being careful not to burn.

Add the coriander, garam masala, turmeric and salt and simmer for about 5 minutes.

Meanwhile, wash the vegetables and chop into 2.5-cm / 1-in pieces; with the green peppers be sure to remove the white pith and the seeds. Add them to the pot and stir in well. Turn them over for about 5 minutes and then add the coconut purée and the green chilli. Bring the whole mixture to the boil and simmer, covered, for about 15 minutes.

Serve sprinkled with the chopped coriander.

BHAGARE BAIGAN

SERVES 4

This dish is another proof of how vegetarian cooks can make the same vegetable taste completely different but still allow it to retain its original fresh taste. Bhagare baigan makes use of the sourness of tamarind to offset the sweetish taste of the aubergine.

625 g / 1½ lb aubergines (round variety)
vegetable or mustard oil
2 large onions, sliced
1 teaspoon mustard seeds
100 g / 4 oz ghee
1½ teaspoons ground coriander
1 green chilli
½ teaspoon chilli powder
1 tablespoon desiccated coconut
3 cloves garlic, chopped
1 teaspoon turmeric
1 teaspoon garam masala
100 g / 4 oz tamarind
1 teaspoon sugar
3 bay leaves

Wash and trim the aubergines and cut into quarters. Heat some oil in a heavy frying pan and sauté the aubergine until the skins just begin to turn crisp and brown. Remove from the pan and put on one side.

Fry the onions and mustard seeds in the ghee in a large saucepan until golden brown, then add the coriander and the chilli. Cook for 5 minutes. Add the chilli powder, coconut, garlic, turmeric and garam masala and fry for a further 3 minutes.

Soak the tamarind in a little hot water and after about 10 minutes squeeze this out and add the water, together with the sugar. Stir well and add the aubergines. Cover and cook for 10 to 15 minutes until the aubergines are tender, stirring occasionally with care to keep the aubergines whole.

Fry the bay leaves in a little oil, and pour on to the top of the dish just before serving.

Top right: _Bhagare Baigan;_ below left: _Onion Pakora (page 43)_

MATAR PANIR

SERVES 4

(Illustrated on page 30)

Of all the savoury dishes with cream cheese, the most popular is matar panir. It is quite easy to make at home once you have prepared the cream cheese.

*whey remaining from
making panir (see below)
225 g/8 oz panir
100 g/4 oz ghee
½ teaspoon salt
2 large onions, sliced
150 ml/¼ pint water
225 g/8 oz frozen peas
½ teaspoon paprika
½ teaspoon ground ginger
½ teaspoon garam masala*

Cut the panir into 1-cm/½-in cubes and fry in the ghee until they are a light brown colour. Remove from the ghee and leave to soak for 15 minutes in the whey and the salt.

Fry the onions in the same ghee until golden brown. Remove the onions and keep to one side.

Add the water to the pot and then the peas. Cover and cook for about 3–4 minutes until the peas are almost cooked and then drain.

Add the onions, panir cubes, paprika and ginger and stir very gently for 2 to 3 minutes.

Add the garam masala, stirring for 2 minutes and serve immediately.

PANIR

*1.15 litres/2 pints milk
1 tablespoon lemon juice or 4
tablespoons natural yogurt*

Place the milk in a large saucepan and bring to the boil, stirring continuously so that no skin forms on top of the milk. When the milk boils, remove from the heat and while allowing it to cool, gradually add the lemon juice or yogurt, stirring all the time until the milk has curdled completely.

Cover and leave for 15 minutes.

Strain through a muslin cloth, squeezing well to extract all the watery whey. The loose curds left in the cloth are known as chenna. This is the form usually used for making sweets.

However, some savoury recipes call for cubes of Indian cream cheese, and so to obtain these it is necessary to compress the chenna into a slab to form panir. This is done by wrapping the curds in a cloth and compressing between a few old books so there is a weight of approximately 3.25 kg/7 lb on the cheese. You will find that the cheese will have compressed into a slab after about 2½ hours. This slab can then be cut into cubes and stored in a refrigerator.

BAIGAN BOORTHA

SERVES 4

(Illustrated on page 26)

Boortha is a typically Muslim dish which is often served with palao rice and kitcheree. The taste is more correctly described as savoury rather than the hot spicy taste associated with vegetable curries. As such, it provides an interesting alternative to the usual vegetable dishes served alongside Indian meals. As with most other styles of cooking all manner of vegetables can be used and the following recipe uses aubergines which is one of the best tasting vegetables when cooked in this way.

*450 g/1 lb aubergines
1 large onion, finely chopped
2 green chillies
1 tablespoon desiccated coconut
1 teaspoon sesame seed oil
1 teaspoon salt
2 teaspoons lemon juice
chopped parsley to garnish*

Boil the aubergines in salted water or bake in a medium oven.

When they are fully tender remove the skins and mash the aubergines into a pulp and add the onion together with the green chillies.

Transfer the pulp into a saucepan and gently cook for about 3 minutes.

Add the desiccated coconut together with the sesame seed oil, salt and lemon juice. Cook for 10 minutes and serve sprinkled with chopped parsley.

KHAT MITHI GOBI
SERVES 4

Whenever sourness is required in a dish, it is usual to add tomatoes. This may seem strange to us in the West where tomatoes are usually sweet, but the variety that is grown in India has a very sour taste. Unfortunately this type of tomato is not usually available in the West and so it is necessary to use vinegar to obtain the sharp flavour, but keeping the tomatoes to retain the consistency.

100 g / 4 oz carrots, grated
225 g / 8 oz firm tomatoes, sliced
175 g / 6 oz ghee
1½ tablespoons vinegar
50 g / 2 oz sugar
1½ teaspoons salt
1½ teaspoons cornflour
350 g / 12 oz cabbage

Fry the carrots and tomatoes in about half the ghee until tender. This should take about 5 minutes.

Press through a sieve into a large saucepan and add the vinegar, sugar, and salt.

Make the cornflour into a paste with a little water and add to the pan. Bring to the boil, stirring constantly.

Wash the cabbage well and separate the leaves, cutting into 2.5-cm / 1-in strips. Melt the rest of the ghee in a large frying pan and fry the strips of cabbage on high heat for 5 minutes until tender.

Pour the sauce over the cabbage; boil for a further 2 minutes and serve.

GOBI MUSALLUM
SERVES 4

I always feel that this dish is best taken on a cold winter's night as it really does warm the 'cockles of your heart'.

25 g / 1 oz tamarind
150 ml / ¼ pint water
1 teaspoon chilli powder
1½ teaspoons ground coriander
1 cauliflower
50 g / 2 oz desiccated coconut
150 ml / ¼ pint milk
½ teaspoon salt

Top: *Gobi Musallum*; below: *Khat Mithi Gobi*

Soak the tamarind for approximately 4 hours in the water. Then squeeze out the husk and retain only the water.

Place this water in a heavy-based saucepan and mix in the chilli powder and coriander.

Wash the cauliflower well and remove all bruises and blemishes and divide into small sprigs. Add to the pot and begin to cook on a low heat.

Add the desiccated coconut to the milk, mixing well and pour into the saucepan.

Add the salt, cover and simmer gently for 20 minutes. It is important to ensure that the mixture does not dry up during cooking. Add a little water if necessary. Turn the cauliflower occasionally to ensure that the spices permeate well.

DUM ARVI

SERVES 4

This recipe makes use of yams, a vegetable very common throughout India and the West Indies. For general use, yams are prepared in a similar way to potatoes, but as they tend to be a little more glutinous and starchy it is necessary, after having peeled the yams, to soak them for about an hour in salted water to remove the excess starch. In central India where yams grow quite abundantly the yam will often take the place of rice in a meal. Choose only the firm, undamaged yams.

450 g/1 lb yams
100 g/4 oz ghee
1 small onion, sliced
½ teaspoon ground ginger
1 teaspoon ground coriander
½ teaspoon garam masala
½ teaspoon paprika
2 teaspoons salt
2 green chillies, chopped
Garnish
chopped parsley
little butter

Wash and peel the yams and soak for an hour in salted water. Remove and wash off the jelly-like outer coating that forms and pat dry. Chop roughly into 2.5-cm/1-in cubes and fry in the ghee. Remove and place to one side. Fry the onion in the remaining ghee. Stir in the ginger, coriander, garam masala, paprika, salt and the green chillies.

Cover with a loose-fitting lid and place in a moderate oven (180C, 350F, gas 4) for 1 hour. After this the yams should be almost dry and beautifully tender.

Serve garnished with the parsley and a little butter.

CABBAGE FOOGATH

SERVES 4

A foogath is the name given to a dish which utilises pre-cooked vegetables. It is therefore a very good way of using up the greens from a Sunday roast, and it is one of the quickest methods of 'currying-up' a vegetable.

1 large onion, sliced
2 cloves garlic, sliced
2 green chillies, sliced
100 g/4 oz ghee
450 g/1 lb cooked cabbage
1 teaspoon garam masala
ground ginger
1 teaspoon salt
desiccated coconut to garnish

Fry the onion with the garlic and chillies in the ghee until the onions are golden brown.

Add the cabbage with the garam masala, ground ginger and salt and stir on a medium heat until the cabbage is heated right through and becomes very dry. Serve garnished with desiccated coconut.

Note Try adding a variety of cooked vegetables to the above dish if you do not have a great deal of cabbage leftover. Cubed cooked potatoes, cooked peas, cut up, cooked Brussels sprouts, cubed parsnips and carrots are all suitable.

BAIGAN BHUGIA

SERVES 4

A bhugia is the name given to any vegetable dish cooked without any water. This means the dish calls for some care in preparation and that the final result is very dry. Any number of different types of vegetable can be used in a bhugia and the following recipe makes use of two vegetables, the green pepper or pimento and aubergines. The dish tends to be rather hot but this can be controlled by altering the amount of paprika or chillies.

50 g/2 oz ghee
1 large onion, chopped
225 g/8 oz aubergines, long variety
225 g/8 oz green peppers
1½ teaspoons salt
1 teaspoon paprika
2 small green chillies
50 g/2 oz tomato purée
1 teaspoon garam masala

Heat the ghee in a heavy-based saucepan and add the onion. Cook for a few minutes, stirring occasionally.

Left: *Cabbage Foogath*; right: *Baigan Bhugia*

Remove the leafy stem of the aubergines and cut into 1-cm/½-in cubes.

Cut the green peppers in half, remove the seeds and chop coarsely. Add, with the aubergine, to the onion and cook for 5 minutes, stirring constantly.

Add the salt, paprika and chillies. Cover and simmer for a further 10 minutes.

Stir in the tomato purée and the garam masala and simmer for another 5 minutes. Transfer to a heated serving dish and serve immediately.

Note For a simple, spicy vegetarian meal serve the aubergine and green pepper dish with freshly cooked Parathas (page 60) or Palao Rice (page 57).

Side Dishes

No Indian meal is complete without, at the least, a small bowl of natural yogurt. In this chapter you will find a few interesting dishes which you may like to include as part of an Indian meal.

If you're feeling quite adventurous you may like to attempt Kela Kofta – a dish of green banana balls cooked with onion, garlic, spices, cream and tomato purée. Egyptian lentils are available from health food shops as well as from specialist Indian stores and they are used in Kabli Chenna, one of the many dals that are prepared all over India. This dish can be served instead of rice or it would also make an interesting and nutritious vegetarian dish.

For a refreshing change, you may like to make the Indian answer to salad – Cachumber. Ginger, raw onion and lemon juice make this a refreshing and quite different side dish.

CACHUMBER
SERVES 4

Cachumber is basically an Indian way of dressing up a salad. It makes use of ginger and raw onion to provide a piquant flavour. To those unused to eating Indian food it provides a cool refreshment to a hot curry. There are no rules for making cachumber – the following recipe may be added to or subtracted from depending on the vegetables available.

*50 g/2 oz fresh root ginger, peeled
and sliced or
25 g/1 oz ground ginger
225 g/8 oz tomatoes, chopped
juice of 2 lemons
1½ teaspoons salt
1 small onion, sliced
2 tablespoons olive oil
1 tablespoon vinegar*

Mix the ginger, tomatoes, lemon juice and salt.
Gradually pour in the oil and vinegar.
Leave refrigerated in an airtight container until needed for use. Cachumber is always best when chilled, used straight from the refrigerator.

CUCUMBER RAETA
SERVES 4

(Illustrated on page 24)

Raeta is a very suitable antidote to a hot curry. Raeta is the general name for any yogurt-based cooked vegetable or fruit dish which is served to accompany a meal, preferably chilled. There is no limit to the many different varieties that can be made. The most popular recipes make use of bananas, potatoes, raw aubergines and mint. Cucumber raeta is the most famous in the West.

*2.5-cm/1-in length cucumber
300 ml/½ pint natural yogurt
½ teaspoon salt*
Garnish
*1 teaspoon dried mint
½ teaspoon paprika*

Slice the cucumber in the normal way and cut each slice into narrow strips or dice.
Mix these strips into the yogurt with the salt.
Sprinkle with the mint and paprika, and serve chilled in large quantities.

Top: *Cachumber*; below: *Mushroom Palao*
(page 56)

KELA KOFTA
SERVES 4

This recipe makes use of green bananas which may be difficult to obtain. This is an exotic and different dish which has no counterpart in Western cuisine.

675 g/1½ lb green bananas
75 g/3 oz ghee
1 small onion, sliced
2 cloves garlic, chopped
½ teaspoon ground ginger
1 teaspoon salt
1 teaspoon paprika
3 cardamom seeds
1 egg
150 ml/¼ pint single cream
75 g/3 oz tomato purée
pinch of salt
1 tablespoon ghee
chopped fresh coriander to garnish

Boil the bananas for about 10 minutes in their skins until they become tender. Remove from the heat and allow to cool, then remove the skins and mash the bananas thoroughly.

Heat the ghee and fry the onion, garlic and ginger.

Add the banana pulp along with the salt, paprika, and cardamoms, stirring well. Allow to cool.

Mix in the egg until you have a soft, pliable dough; shape the mixture into balls approximately 2.5 cm/1 in. in diameter and place on one side.

Place the cream and tomato purée in a saucepan together with a pinch of salt and a little ghee and simmer, stirring constantly. Add the koftas to this mixture and heat gently until ready to serve. Garnish with coriander.

Kitcheree (page 55)

KABLI CHENNA
SERVES 4

This recipe make use of whole Bengal beans, otherwise known as Egyptian lentils. It is just one of the many dals that are served all over India, but in my opinion it is the most tasty and also the easiest to prepare as it uses just a pinch each of the usual Indian ingredients.

225 g/8 oz Egyptian lentils
600 ml/1 pint water
1 small onion, sliced
1 clove garlic, chopped
50 g/2 oz ghee
1 teaspoon ground coriander
1 teaspoon turmeric
½ teaspoon ground cumin
½ teaspoon chilli powder
1 teaspoon fenugreek
little vinegar to mix

Wash the lentils well, using four or five changes of water. Boil for approximately 10 minutes in lightly salted water. The lentils should just begin to be tender.

Fry the onion and garlic in the ghee in the bottom of a heavy-based saucepan.

While the onions and the garlic are frying, mix the remaining powdered ingredients into a stiff paste with a little vinegar, then add the paste to the pan and fry for a further 3 or 4 minutes.

Drain the lentils and add to the pan; heat gently for 10 minutes.

Serve immediately.

Rice Dishes

Delicately scented Basmati rice flavoured with mild spices makes a standard accompaniment for most Indian dishes. Here you will find a recipe for plain Palao Rice and another richer recipe for Kesari Chaval which includes plenty of ghee, saffron and onions.

Kitcheree is the dish from which the idea for that favourite breakfast dish, kedgeree, originated. Consisting of Basmati rice and yellow moong dal, this authentic spicy recipe is served with hard-boiled eggs and onions mixed in.

Another particularly interesting recipe, which illustrates the versatile nature of Indian rice recipes, is Hoppers. In this case the best Basmati rice is ground with coconut milk to make a batter, then cooked as delicious pancakes.

There are one or two basic points to remember when cooking rice. Firstly, the type is important and Basmati rice is best. Wash the rice carefully first, swilling it gently in a bowl of water, draining and rinsing again. Take care not to damage the grains as they will burst during cooking.

KESARI CHAVAL
SERVES 4

Saffron rice is the beautiful yellow rice that is nearly always served in Indian restaurants, often under the name of palao. However, to lump it with the other forms of rice would be doing it a grave injustice; this rice stands in a class of its own. It certainly makes an eye-catching centre piece at a dinner party.

225 g/8 oz Basmati rice
½ teaspoon saffron
2 tablespoons boiling water
100 g/4 oz ghee
2.5-cm/1-in piece cinnamon stick
3 cloves
2 large onions, sliced
600 ml/1 pint water
1 teaspoon salt
2 cardamom seeds
silver leaf to garnish

Wash the rice well and then drain thoroughly.

Place the saffron in a small cup and pour over it about 2 tablespoons of boiling water. Soak for about 10 minutes.

While the saffron is soaking put the ghee in a heavy pot and then add the cinnamon, cloves and onions. Fry for about 10 minutes, turning constantly to ensure that none of the ingredients stick to the pan.

Turn the heat to very low and add the rice stirring for about 5 minutes until each grain of rice has the same delicate, golden yellow colour.

Meanwhile, boil the water, together with the salt and cardamom seeds. Add this to the rice and bring rapidly to the boil again. Reduce the heat and add the saffron, together with the water in which it has been soaking and stir in gently. Cover and simmer for 25 minutes until the rice has absorbed all the liquid.

Serve garnished with silver leaf.

KITCHEREE

SERVES 4

(Illustrated on previous page)

Kitcheree is a dish prepared with rice and lentils. It must be stressed that any spicing is to enhance the flavour of these two ingredients. The following recipe is a general one, making use of the yellow moong dal variety of lentils.

225 g/8 oz Basmati rice
225 g/8 oz yellow moong dal
1 clove garlic, sliced
5 cloves
5 cardamom seeds
5-cm/2-in piece cinnamon stick
75 g/3 oz ghee
1 small onion, sliced
1 teaspoon turmeric
$\frac{1}{2}$ teaspoon salt
Garnish
hard-boiled egg or fried onion rings
chopped fresh coriander

Mix the rice and dal together and wash thoroughly in cold water using at least five changes of water. Pick out all the stones and other bits and pieces. Allow to soak in cold water for 1 hour.

Left: *Kela Kofta;* right: *Kabli Chenna (both recipes on page 53)*

Fry the garlic, cloves, cardamoms and cinnamon in the ghee in a large saucepan with a close-fitting lid for 1 minute.

Add the onion and fry for a further minute in the ghee but do not allow the onion to brown.

Drain the rice and lentils and add to the saucepan, together with the turmeric and salt. Toss all this gently using a wooden spoon over a very low heat for about 4 or 5 minutes.

Boil some water sufficient to cover the rice and when the 4 to 5 minutes are up, add this boiling water and cover the rice plus about 2.5 cm/1 in.

Cover with a lid and simmer for approximately 30–45 minutes so that all the moisture is absorbed and the rice is cooked.

Serve garnished with slices of hard-boiled egg, or fried onion rings and freshly chopped coriander.

MUSHROOM PALAO

SERVES 4

(Illustrated on page 51)

This recipe is very similar to that for ordinary palao rice, but remember that in order to preserve the delicate flavour of the mushrooms they must not be over-cooked.

50 g/2 oz ghee
2 medium onions, sliced
6 cardamom seeds · 6 cloves
1 teaspoon cumin seeds
1 teaspoon black peppercorns
1 teaspoon salt
225 g/8 oz mushrooms, chopped
450 g/1 lb Basmati rice
1.15 litres/2 pints water

Place the ghee into a large saucepan over a medium heat. Fry the onions adding the cardamoms, cloves, cumin seeds, peppercorns and salt after about a minute. Continue to fry, stirring well for about 2 minutes.

Add the mushrooms. The pan should be shaken not stirred as stirring would tend to break the mushrooms. Fry for about 2 minutes. Now remove the mushrooms using a perforated spoon, trying to avoid removing the spices.

Add the washed rice to the saucepan immediately followed by the water. Bring to the boil, cover and cook gently for 15 minutes. By this time a lot of the water should have been absorbed.

Add the mushrooms stirring in gently and continue to cook until the rice is soft.

Drain off any excess water. Keep in a hot oven until you are ready to serve the meal. A damp cloth over the top of the rice will prevent the rice drying out on the surface.

Hoppers (page 63)

PALAO RICE

SERVES 4

(Illustrated on front cover)

Those of you who eat regularly in Indian restaurants may be somewhat confused as to what is and what is not palao rice. This is because some less scrupulous restaurants serve up plain boiled rice that has been coloured bright yellow under the title of palao rice. In fact, true palao rice needs to be cooked in a particular way and has no added colouring. The idea is to bring out the flavour of the rice itself by adding small amounts of other flavourings such as cloves, cumin seeds and cardamoms.

450 g/1 lb Basmati rice
50 g/2 oz ghee
2 medium onions, sliced
6 cloves
6 cardamom seeds
1 teaspoon black peppercorns
1 teaspoon cumin seeds
½ teaspoon salt
1.15 litres/2 pints water

Wash the rice well and then drain thoroughly.

Place the ghee in a large saucepan over a medium heat. Fry the onions in the ghee for about a minute.

Add the cloves, cardamoms, peppercorns and cumin seeds together with the salt. Fry for a further 2 minutes.

Reduce the heat and add the rice immediately followed by the water. Bring to the boil and cook gently until the rice is soft, about 20 to 30 minutes.

Drain off any excess water and place in a hot oven covered with a damp tea towel until ready to serve.

DOSA

SERVES 4

Dosas are similar to pancakes; however, they are made in a slightly different way, using whole rice and urad dal instead of the plain flour used in Western-style pancakes. They are usually made very thin and filled with a dry vegetable mixture and served rolled up and sprinkled with paprika and lemon juice. The potato-based filling is just one of many that can be made and any dry vegetable or meat dish can be used.

50 g/2 oz rice
175 g/6 oz urad dal
600 ml/1 pint water
pinch of bicarbonate of soda
1 teaspoon chilli powder
vegetable oil
Filling
1 kg/2 lb potatoes, peeled
4 tablespoons vegetable oil
2 teaspoons mustard seeds
6 curry leaves, crushed
1 teaspoon salt
½ teaspoon turmeric
½ teaspoon chilli powder
2 large onions, sliced
225 g/8 oz tomatoes, chopped
150 ml/¼ pint water
Garnish
wedges of lemon
paprika

Wash the rice and dal well and soak overnight in about 600 ml/1 pint of water. Blend in a liquidiser to the consistency of condensed milk. Beat in the bicarbonate of soda and the chilli powder and allow to stand for 15 minutes.

In a heavy-based frying pan, fry like conventional pancakes ensuring that the vegetable oil is very hot. When cooked remove and keep hot.

Chop the potatoes into 2.5-cm/1-in cubes. Heat the vegetable oil in a heavy-based saucepan until it is almost smoking. Add the mustard seeds and when they begin to burst, cover the pan to prevent the seeds from popping everywhere.

Add the curry leaves, salt, turmeric, and chilli powder and stir for 2 minutes. Add the potatoes and fry gently for 1 minute. Add the onions, tomatoes and water and simmer for 10 minutes until the potatoes are soft. If necessary, evaporate any excess liquid to produce a dry mixture.

Fill each pancake with the mixture. Serve garnished with lemon and sprinkled with paprika.

Breads & Snacks

A particular characteristic of the Indian way of eating is the frequent partaking of snacks and probably the best known of these are crisp pasties, known as samosas.

Light, puffed breads are served with meals instead of or as well as rice. They are broken and used to mop up juices and gravy. It is important that the various breads are all cooked just before they are served for they are at their best only when freshly made.

Among the other snacks in this chapter you will find Dosas – pancakes made from a batter prepared from a mixture of rice and lentils. Filled or served plain these are satisfying and delicious.

When you are planning an Indian meal, then try and include these recipes as part of the menu. You may even find that some of these snacks make a very good opening course if you are serving the meal in several separate courses.

PAKORA

SERVES 4

(Illustrated on page 62)

I have heard the pakora described in many ways, perhaps the most apt being that it is like a spiced Yorkshire pudding with a filling. Pakoras may be made of many things, but the most essential thing is the batter. Gram flour is much finer than our flour and forms lumps easier. Thus it should be well sifted and the batter beaten constantly. You can fill pakoras with almost any vegetable or fruit but the most tasty are the ones made from thin slices of aubergine (*baigan pakora*), and those made from spinach (*saag pakora*).

Batter
1 medium onion, chopped roughly
¼ lemon, chopped roughly
300 ml/½ pint natural yogurt
1 teaspoon chilli powder
½ teaspoon mustard powder
150–175 g/5–6 oz gram or chick-pea flour, sifted
Fillings
3-mm/⅛ in aubergine slices
vegetable oil
spinach leaves

Place the onion and lemon with the yogurt in a liquidiser and blend to a smooth sauce. Pour this out into a large mixing bowl and add the chilli powder and mustard.

Add the flour gradually until the batter forms small peaks which disintegrate 15 or 20 seconds later. Depending on how liquid the yogurt is, you may have to add more or less gram flour. This batter will keep for weeks if it is covered and placed in a refrigerator. It is also quite easy to freeze – very useful if you ever want teatime snacks in a hurry.

For the filling, dip the aubergine slices into the batter and deep-fry in clean cooking oil. If it is too hot you will find that the pakoras go very dark brown on the outside and stay soft and stodgy inside; if the oil is too cool they will be laden with fat when taken out. If in doubt, follow the manufacturer's recommended temperature for fritters.

When using spinach or any other sort of leaf, it is essential to ensure that the leaves are dry, otherwise the frying oil will deteriorate very quickly.

CHAPATTYS

SERVES 4

As in rice cooking the secret of the chapatty does not lie so much in the cooking as in the basic ingredients. A lot of the major cities nowadays have Indian delicatessens and even one or two of the larger milling firms make their own special brand of flour, known as chapatty flour or *ata*. It is a mistake to make chapattys with wholemeal flour as I have tried and the result is far too starchy.

$\frac{1}{2}$ *teaspoon salt*
225 g/8 oz chapatty flour
little water

Add the salt to the chapatty flour and gradually add the water until you obtain an homogeneous dough which is wet to the touch. The dough, however, should be quite firm and hard.

To make one chapatty break off a piece of the dough about 5 cm/2 in. in diameter and roll in some dry flour. Place the ball on a floured board and roll into a disc about 15 cm/6 in. in diameter. The chapatty should be about 3 mm/$\frac{1}{8}$ in thick.

Flour a tawa or equivalent lightly. It should be so hot that when water is thrown on it, it spatters

Left: Chapattys; right: Puris (overleaf)

immediately. Take the chapatty and lay it over the top of the tawa for 45 seconds and then turn it and cook for a further 45 seconds.

Move the tawa to one side and place the chapatty on the naked heat source if electric or under the grill of an electric or gas cooker. The chapatty will swell out and one or two small burnt patches will appear.

Serve at the table wrapped in a warm cloth.

Note Indians cook chapattys on a hemispherical iron plate placed over the heat source called a *tawa*. A compromise is an upturned frying pan or a griddle. Chapattys should always be eaten fresh as a re-warmed chapatty is like leather. This fact is worth bearing in mind when you have guests and are trying to decide whether to have rice or some form of bread; the rice will release you for your guests whereas you will have to cook right up to the last minute if you choose one of the breads.

PARATHAS
SERVES 4

Parathas are perhaps more simple to make than the ordinary chapatty as the cooking technique is similar to Western customs. The paratha is slightly larger in diameter and about twice as thick as the chapatty; therefore the preceding ingredients will make half the number of parathas. Do not forget of course that the bread will be twice as filling.

225 g/8 oz chapatty flour
pinch of salt
little water
100 g/4 oz ghee

Take a 10-cm/4-in ball of dough, coat in flour and roll it out as thinly as possible on a floured board.

With a pastry brush paint the melted ghee all over the upper surface of the dough. Now fold the paratha and reform into a round ball. Roll this out to a disc 15 cm/6 in wide and 5 mm–1 cm/$\frac{1}{4}$–$\frac{1}{2}$ in thick.

Pour a little of the melted ghee into the hot frying pan and fry the paratha on both sides until it is crisp on the outside. Serve hot.

PURI
SERVES 4

(Illustrated on previous page)

Puri is in essence a deep-fried chapatty with the addition of ghee in the dough. Puris are traditionally served at breakfast with coffee, but they are equally apt at an evening meal. The ingredients here will make approximately 12 puris as they are thinner than chapattys.

100 g/4 oz ghee
225 g/8 oz chapatty flour
little water
vegetable oil

Rub the ghee into the flour and then make a chapatty-like dough by gradually adding water.

Break off 2.5-cm/1-in pieces and roll out to 13-cm/5-in discs.

Heat the oil and drop the puri in carefully to avoid creasing it. If the oil is the right temperature the puri will immediately puff up into a ball and float to the surface. Push it underneath until it is crisp on both sides. Lift it out, drain off excess oil and store in a warm dish.

SAMOSA
MAKES ABOUT 50

Samosas are the Indian equivalent of the Cornish pasty, being originally designed as a convenient way of carrying meat and in some cases, a sweet dish, for the midday meal. The recipe here is for the pastry which is the essential part. The most popular filling for samosa in India consists of peas, potatoes and minced meat.

100 g/4 oz margarine
225 g/8 oz plain flour
$\frac{1}{2}$ teaspoon salt
1 teaspoon black cumin seeds
(optional)
150 ml/$\frac{1}{4}$ pint milk
vegetable oil

Rub the margarine into the flour together with the salt and cumin seeds (if used), so that the flour has an homogeneous consistency.

Add the milk and mix until you have a dough which is hard and slightly tacky to the touch. Add more milk or flour as necessary.

Break off 2.5-cm/1-in balls of dough and roll them on a floury board until you have circles 1.5 mm/$\frac{1}{16}$ in thick. Repeat this process until you have 25 rounds of pastry.

Lay the rounds one on the top of the other making sure each is well floured to prevent sticking. With a sharp knife cut into semi-circles.

Have by your side a bowl of flour and a bowl of cold water. Take a semi-circle of pastry and lay it across your right hand. Place about 1 tablespoon of the cooked filling in the centre. Fold over one corner of the semi-circle to form a cone shape and glue the seam with a little water. Close the top by pressing together the moistened edges.

Fry in a small deep frying pan for about a minute in vegetable oil until golden brown. Samosas may be served either hot or cold.

Note Fill the samosas with a mixture of 225 g/8 oz minced beef cooked with about 225 g/8 oz diced potatoes and 100 g/4 oz frozen peas. Add 1 teaspoon garam masala and 1 teaspoon mustard seeds then cool before use. Alternatively increase the quantities of vegetables and omit the meat.

Samosas

HOPPERS
MAKES ABOUT 8
(Illustrated on page 56)

Hoppers are very similar to dosas and they are a typical Madras dish. Originally hoppers were cooked in earthenware pots with rounded bottoms known as *hopper-chattis*, which were placed in the ashes of a slow charcoal fire. The hopper batter would be poured in and the chatti quickly spun to make the batter swirl around into the hotter parts of the vessel. This would give a lacy crisp border to the pancake. The centre of the hopper is somewhat thicker than the dosa. This method of cooking is a very skilful one, but it is something that can be emulated in the Western kitchen by using a small omelette pan and swirling the batter so that it runs up the sides. Alternatively, one can use a metal *kurhai* which has two handles to facilitate the swirling process. These kurhais are completely curved and can be bought in either Chinese or Indian shops.

225 g/8 oz Basmati rice
1 teaspoon salt
150 ml/¼ pint coconut milk
pinch of bicarbonate of soda
little butter

Grind the rice using a coffee mill or a mortar and pestle, and mix together with the salt and the coconut milk and a pinch of bicarbonate of soda. Leave overnight. In the morning whip the batter so that there is plenty of air in it. This has the effect of making the hoppers light.

Grease the cooking vessel with a little butter. Place over a medium heat and pour in a little of the batter. Spin immediately so that the batter runs up the side.

As soon as the batter hardens in the middle, remove with a fish slice. Store in a warm cloth. Hoppers are usually eaten at breakfast or teatime.

Top: *Chaat (page 72)*; below: *Pakoras (page 58)*

GOL GUPPAS
SERVES 4

A favourite western India teatime snack is a gol guppa. Traditionally gol guppas have always been sold on the sea-shore at Bombay, usually with zeera pani, tamarind water. The gol guppa is roughly 2.5 cm/1 in. in diameter and wafer thin. In India people eat them like chips or crisps in the West. Gol guppas are easily made but must be eaten freshly cooked. They are also easily made in quantity and are therefore ideal for a party.

100 g/4 oz plain flour
100 g/4 oz semolina
100 g/4 oz urad dal
150 ml/¼ pint water
ghee for frying

Sieve the flour and semolina into a bowl. Grind the urad dal to a powder and add to the bowl.

Form into a hard dough with the water. Knead for 15 minutes; set aside in a wet cloth for 20 minutes.

Divide the dough into small pieces about the size of a gooseberry, roll into small balls, using the hands, and then roll out flat as thinly as possible, dusting whenever necessary with a little flour.

Heat the ghee and deep-fry the gol guppas for about 2 minutes until they puff up. Remove and place on absorbent kitchen paper.

Serve cold with Zeera pani (see below).

ZEERA PANI
SERVES 4

100 g/4 oz tamarind
600 ml/1 pint water
2 teaspoons cumin seeds
1 teaspoon paprika
4 teaspoons salt
2 teaspoons sugar
1.15 litres/2 pints water
juice of ½ lemon

Soak the tamarind overnight in the water. Strain and add the remaining ingredients and the lemon juice. Mix well and refrigerate for 2 hours.

To fill gol guppas make a small hole in the top of each one with a finger and arrange on a dish. Pour the zeera pani into each and serve immediately.

Desserts & Drinks

After a spicy curry, a simple, cooling dessert can be very welcome. Try making Pista Kulfi, an Indian ice cream, or serve a bowl of Chaat which is a spicy fruit salad.

More substantial desserts in the form of rich Meeta Palao, a sweet palao rice, or Rasagulla, sweet cream cheese balls, make an interesting final course to the meal. If you are serving such dishes, then try to avoid overloading your guests in the main course by serving light dishes.

Lastly, refreshing drinks are always welcome with a spicy curry. The most common is probably Lassi (a yogurt-based drink) and it is well worth trying.

When you've mastered the art of making Indian sweetmeats, then you can feel confident that your repertoire of dishes is quite good enough to prepare a feast. A little advance preparation will make for a memorable meal.

KULFI MALAI

SERVES 4

(Illustrated on page 73)

In general Indian sweets are not well known in the West, especially the more difficult ones such as kulfi malai. Much has been made of the French and Italian ice creams, but in my opinion this mango ice cream is the most exquisite I have ever had. Although some of the ingredients are a little difficult to obtain it is in fact quite simple to make.

350-g/12-oz can condensed milk
300 ml/½ pint double cream
100 g/4 oz granulated sugar
1 tablespoon grated almonds
1 tablespoon grated pistachios
350-g/12-oz can mango slices or pulp
1 tablespoon kewra water
finely beaten silver foil to decorate

Boil the milk and the cream together with the sugar stirring constantly and leave to simmer on a very low heat for 30 minutes.

Add the almonds and pistachios, stirring in well and cool to room temperature by standing the saucepan in running cold water.

Add the mango pulp or crushed slices. If using the latter it is necessary to drain off half the juice from the can. Add the kewra water.

Mix the preparation well with a wire whisk and place to set in moulds. These may be any shape you like, but traditionally the kulfi wallahs of India use conical aluminium moulds with screw tops.

Place the moulds in the freezer and the kulfi will be ready when solid. As this recipe contains no artificial gelling agents you will find that on removal from the freezer it will melt very quickly. It is therefore necessary to keep the moulds in the refrigerator until serving.

Note In India this dish is always decorated with very finely beaten, edible silver foil, known as *varak*. It is well worth the extra expense if you can get hold of it in Indian shops.

KHEER

SERVES 4

(Illustrated on page 70)

Kheer is essentially a rice pudding but it is far superior to the one eaten in the West. It is a great favourite for parties as it is best served cold from the fridge.

75 g/3 oz rice
150 ml/¼ pint water
1.75 litres/3 pints milk
175 g/6 oz sugar
2 cardamom seeds, crushed
3–4 drops kewra water
15 g/½ oz blanched almonds
50 g/2 oz raisins
finely beaten silver foil to garnish

Soak the rice in the water for 30 minutes. Bring to the boil and boil until the water dries up.

Add the milk to the saucepan and stir the rice, keeping on a very low heat for 1½ hours. During cooking keep scraping the bottom and sides of the pan until you have a creamy consistency and then add the sugar.

When you have a perfect consistency remove from the heat and add the crushed cardamoms, kewra water, almonds and raisins.

Pour into small dishes and allow to set in the fridge.

Note In India, kheer and other sweet dishes are usually served decorated with very thin leaves of pure silver. If you can get hold of some from your local Indian suppliers then your kheer will be that much more attractive – not to say more expensive. This silver foil is not only edible but some people believe that it is an aid to digestion.

In the goblet: *Lassi (page 75);* on the tray: *Bombay Halwa (page 72)*

MEETA PALAO

SERVES 4

Literally translated, meeta palao means sweet rice, and as you would expect this dish takes the form of ordinary rice with added flavour. Meeta palao is an inexpensive sweet to prepare and can be served either hot or cold. All the ingredients are readily obtainable.

450 g/1 lb Basmati rice
225 g/8 oz ghee
6 cloves
6 cardamom seeds
5-cm/2-in piece cinnamon stick
100 g/4 oz sultanas
50 g/2 oz blanched almonds
50 g/2 oz pistachios
½ teaspoon saffron
150 ml/¼ pint water
100 g/4 oz castor sugar
Decoration
blanched almonds
pistachios

Wash the rice well and soak in cold water for 2 hours.

Melt the ghee in a heavy-based pan and fry the cloves, cardamoms, and cinnamon for 2 or 3 minutes. Add the sultanas, almonds and pistachios and fry for a further 2 or 3 minutes.

Meanwhile soak the saffron in the water. Pour this water together with the saffron into the pan.

Drain the rice and add to the frying pan, turning gently for another 10 minutes.

Add enough hot water to cover the rice, place a tight-fitting lid on the pan and continue to cook slowly until all the water has been absorbed and the rice has been cooked.

Finally stir in the sugar and serve decorated with blanched almonds and pistachios.

Meeta Palao

PAYASAM

SERVES 4

Payasam is another of the Indian milk-based sweets. This dish uses sage to give a creamy consistency along with vermicelli and desiccated coconut. As it is quite complicated to make, it is a dish usually reserved for feast days.

50 g/2 oz sago
300 ml/½ pint water
5 cardamom seeds
1 teaspoon melted ghee
1.15 litres/2 pints milk
50 g/2 oz sugar
50 g/2 oz vermicelli
50 g/2 oz desiccated coconut
50 g/2 oz sultanas
pistachios to garnish

Soak the sago for 1 hour in the water.

Fry the cardamoms in the ghee in a large saucepan and add the milk and sugar.

Bring to the boil, simmer for 10 minutes, stirring constantly to ensure that the sugar is dissolved. Drain the sago and add, stirring for a further 5 minutes.

Add the vermicelli and stir for 2 minutes.

Add the coconut and sultanas and bring to the boil; simmer for 5 minutes.

Serve garnished with pistachios.

RASGULLAH

SERVES 4

Rasgullah is the best and probably the most famous sweet to come out of east India. The recipe calls for the use of panir (see page 46). The success of this dish depends on the special syrup.

1.15 litres/2 pints milk
2 tablespoons lemon juice
1.15 litres/2 pints water
900 g/2 lb sugar
½ lemon, chopped
6 cloves
6 cardamom seeds
2 teaspoons rose water

Make the milk into panir (see page 46) using the lemon juice.

Knead the curds well into little balls about the size of a marble and place on a sheet of greaseproof paper. Put aside.

Prepare the syrup. Boil the water and add the sugar together with the lemon cut into small pieces, the cloves, cardamoms and rose water. Bring to the boil and ensure that the sugar is completely dissolved; boil until you have obtained a heavy syrup.

Allow this to cool and drop the small cheese balls into the syrup. Chill and serve.

Note Rasgullahs can be kept in a refrigerator for quite a long time but should be stored in a closed container as the syrup will take up other smells in the fridge.

SEWAIAN

SERVES 4

(Illustrated on page 70)

Sewaian is a sweet vermicelli dish peculiar to Muslims all over India. On the various religious festivals it is customary for the lady of each Muslim household to prepare this dish and send portions of it to friends and relations, garnished with finely beaten gold or silver. Vermicelli is usually available in most Italian or French grocers as well as Indian stockists.

50 g/2 oz ghee
8 cardamom seeds, crushed
8 cloves, crushed
225 g/8 oz vermicelli
600 ml/1 pint milk
225 g/8 oz sugar
50 g/2 oz almonds, chopped
50 g/2 oz pistachios, chopped
2 teaspoons rose water

Melt the ghee in a heavy-based saucepan, and fry the cardamoms and cloves for 2 minutes.

Add the vermicelli, being careful not to break it. Fry until it is golden brown in colour.

Add the milk and stir gently but thoroughly. Cover the pan and cook on a medium heat for about 10 minutes, stirring occasionally very gently.

When the milk is almost dried up, add the sugar with the almonds, pistachios and rose water. Stir in well and allow to cool. Sewaian can be served either hot or ice-cold.

From the top: *Payasam, Alebele (page 74) and Podina ka Sharbat (page 74)*

PISTA KULFI

SERVES 4

(Illustrated on page 73)

This is probably the best ice cream I have ever tasted and I know that anything that contains pistachios is bound to delight the palate.

350-g/12-oz can condensed milk
300 ml/½ pint double cream
100 g/4 oz castor sugar
2 eggs
2 drops almond essence
2 drops green food colouring
100 g/4 oz pistachios, shelled plus
extra for decoration

Heat the condensed milk in a saucepan and add the double cream with the sugar.

Separate the egg whites and beat until they form peaks.

Beat the yolks into the milk together with the almond essence and the green colouring. Allow this mixture to simmer gently.

Meanwhile, soak the pistachios to make it easy to remove the skins. Chop finely and add to the saucepan, beating in well. Bring to the boil and then refrigerate until the mixture is nearly set.

Remove and fold in the beaten egg whites. Beat well and freeze until firm. Serve decorated with chopped pistachio nuts.

Note To make the dish authentic the ice cream should be frozen in the traditional aluminium cone shapes used by the kulfi wallahs.

JALLEBI

SERVES 4

(Illustrated on page 75)

Jallebi are crisp, round whirls, very sticky but very popular. Jallebis are good as long as they are freshly made but usually those on sale have been lying around too long. However, it is very easy to make them at home as no special ingredients are needed.

350 g/12 oz plain flour
cold water to mix
150 ml/¼ pint natural yogurt
25 g/1 oz dried yeast
450 g/1 lb sugar
600 ml/1 pint water
pinch of saffron
6 cardamom seeds
6 cloves
vegetable oil
icing sugar to decorate

Sift the flour into a bowl and add sufficient cold water along with the yogurt and yeast to form a batter the consistency of double cream. Cover and stand in a warm place for about 4 hours to ferment.

Meanwhile prepare the syrup by dissolving the sugar in the water in a saucepan, together with the saffron, cardamoms and cloves. Bring to the boil and evaporate until a heavy syrup is obtained.

Heat a good amount of oil in a medium-deep frying pan to nearly boiling. With either an icing bag or a narrow funnel, allow the batter to run into the hot oil to form the traditional figure eights or double circle whirls. Cook for about 1 minute, turning constantly, until the jallebi is a light brown colour.

Remove, drain and immerse in the syrup for approximately 5 minutes, so that the syrup runs through the pipes of the jallebi without making the crisp outside become soggy.

Remove from the syrup, drain and dust with icing sugar.

Top: *Sewaian (page 68)*; below: *Kheer (page 65)*

CHAAT

SERVES 6

(Illustrated on page 62)

Chaat is the name given to any fresh fruit salad spiced with chilli, salt, lemon juice and red peppers. It is very popular in the afternoons when tea is taken, the hot spices coupled with the fresh fruit allay the effects of the afternoon heat. Even in the West there is nothing quite so refreshing as a bowl of refrigerated chaat. The following recipe is for a basic chaat using readily available fruits. However, you can use any fruit but they should not be too ripe.

225 g/8 oz mandarin oranges
225 g/8 oz apples
225 g/8 oz bananas
225 g/8 oz guavas
225 g/8 oz pears
100 g/4 oz stoned cherries
2 tablespoons lemon juice
2 teaspoons sugar
1 teaspoon chilli powder
1 teaspoon paprika
1 teaspoon salt
1½ teaspoons ground ginger
1 teaspoon garam masala

Peel the oranges, apples and bananas, and chop coarsely with the guavas, pears and cherries, taking care to remove the stones and pips.

Place the fruit in a bowl and sprinkle the lemon juice over them, mixing well.

Mix the sugar and spices in a dry bowl. Sprinkle these over the fruit pieces, ensuring that it is all well covered.

Refrigerate for approximately 1 hour before serving.

BOMBAY HALWA

SERVES 6

(Illustrated on page 65)

There are many different types of halwa, each purporting to come from a different city. Thus we have Karachi halwa, Dacca halwa and probably the most famous, Bombay halwa. Halwas differ from the standard style of Indian sweet in as much as they are not based entirely on milk. Bombay halwa contains no milk whatsoever. It is, however, reasonably easy to prepare, but do not expect to emulate exactly the 'halwai's' art as I am positive that this is one dish you have to be born into!

350 g/12 oz sugar
300 ml/½ pint water
50 g/2 oz cornflour
juice of 1 lemon
100 g/4 oz unsalted butter
50 g/2 oz cashew nuts, chopped
50 g/2 oz almonds, chopped
50 g/2 oz pistachios, chopped
2 cardamom seeds, crushed

Dissolve the sugar in a saucepan with the water over a low heat. Bring to the boil and boil for about 7–8 minutes to make a light caramel.

Meanwhile, mix the cornflour with a little cold water to form a paste; add to the caramel solution, stirring continuously.

Add the lemon juice and a little of the butter. Continue to cook on a medium heat until the mixture becomes fudge-like in texture – about 5 minutes.

Add the nuts and cardamoms. Pour into a fudge tray and allow to cool.

When cold, cut into the traditional diamond shapes. Halwa will keep indefinitely in an airtight tin. It makes very suitable presents.

Top: *Kulfi Malai (page 64)* below: *Pista Kulfi (page 71)*

PODINA KA SHARBAT

SERVES 4

(Illustrated on page 69)

In India mint forms the basis of a very tasty, cooling beverage. It is essential to use fresh mint when making podina ka sharbat as dried mint does not have the same intensity of flavour.

100 g/4 oz fresh mint
½ teaspoon ground ginger
175 g/6 oz sugar
1 tablespoon lemon juice
900 ml/1½ pints water
crushed ice
fresh mint to decorate

Crush the mint leaves, preferably with a mortar and pestle, but failing that in a liquidiser or coffee grinder; add the ginger, sugar, lemon juice and water.

Then transfer to a liquidiser and blend for 5 minutes.

Strain through a fine cloth, repeating if necessary to obtain a clear green liquid. Podina ka sharbat is best served as a frappé over crushed ice.

Decorate with a few sprigs of fresh mint.

PHIRNI

SERVES 4

Phirni is a very popular sweet and can best be described as a blancmange. It makes use of almonds and pistachios and kewra essence. These give a distinctive Indian flavour. Rice flour can be bought from most Indian delicatessens. Whole rice can be ground if you want to be sure of the quality of the rice.

25 g/1 oz rice
150 ml/¼ pint water
600 ml/1 pint milk
100 g/4 oz sugar
5 drops kewra essence
25 g/1 oz mixed pistachios and almonds
Decoration
almonds
pistachios

Soak the rice for 1½ hours then drain and grind into a paste with the water.

Heat the milk slowly in a saucepan and stir in the rice paste. Stir until the mixture begins to thicken. Remove from the heat and add the sugar.

When the sugar is fully dissolved, bring to the boil and simmer for 2 minutes. Now allow to cool and add the kewra essence and the chopped almonds and pistachios.

Serve chilled either in individual dishes or in a central dish decorated with split almonds and pistachios.

ALEBELE

SERVES 4

(Illustrated on page 69)

This is a Goanese dish, basically a pancake filled with a spiced coconut mixture. It is a very good dish to serve as a teatime snack.

175 g/6 oz plain flour
½ teaspoon salt
2 eggs
600 ml/1 pint milk
Filling
50 g/2 oz sugar
2 teaspoons treacle
175 g/6 oz desiccated coconut
2 teaspoons ground ginger
2 drops aniseed essence
ghee for cooking
Garnish
icing sugar
wedges of lemon

Sieve the flour into a large bowl, together with the salt; beat in the eggs and milk until well blended. Allow this batter to stand for 30 minutes.

Meanwhile, prepare the stuffing by mixing the sugar and treacle in a bowl; add the coconut, ground ginger and aniseed essence and mix well. Leave this on one side.

Melt just enough ghee to cover the bottom of a heavy-based omelette pan. Pour in 2 tablespoons of the batter with a small ladle, tip the pan to spread the batter evenly over the surface and cook for approximately 1 minute on a moderate heat until the pancake begins to brown, turn the pancake over and cook the other side for a minute. Remove from the heat and keep on a warm plate and cook the rest of the pancakes using a little bit of the ghee each time.

Put about 4 tablespoons of the mixture in the centre of each pancake and roll up.

Arrange each alebele on the plate. Dust with icing sugar and serve cold, garnished with wedges of lemon.

Jallebi (page 71)

ALOO KA MITTHAI

SERVES 6–8

This recipe utilises dried instead of fresh milk. This should be of the best full cream variety and can be bought packed as baby food. The dish also utilises potatoes which should be the newest available.

675 g/1½ lb potatoes (preferably new)
450 g/1 lb full cream dried milk
450 g/1 lb sugar
225 g/8 oz ghee
some icing sugar

Wash the potatoes and steam for 15 minutes, remove the skins and mash.

Add the dried milk and sugar and mix well. Cook gently on a very low heat, gradually adding the ghee. Keep stirring and when the ghee is all separated out, transfer to a baking tin. Allow to cool and sprinkle well with icing sugar.

Cut into the traditional diamond shapes and serve. This dish will keep indefinitely in an airtight container.

LASSI

SERVES 4

(Illustrated on page 65)

This is one of those specialities that needs an acquired taste but it is most enjoyable on a very hot day. Lassi can be drunk in two ways, either sweet (meeta) or salted (numkeen). I suggest the sweet one is tried first as the salted drink is really designed for hot climates.

300 ml/½ pint natural yogurt
300 ml/½ pint milk
juice 1 lemon
½ teaspoon kewra essence or rose water
ice cubes
sugar or salt to taste
lemon slices

Place the yogurt, milk, lemon juice and kewra essence into a liquidiser. Rose water can be used if you cannot obtain kewra essence.

Add some ice cubes and blend until the ice cubes have almost disappeared.

Pour into tall glasses and add the sugar or salt to taste.

Serve with a slice of lemon and a drinking straw.

Index